PRAISE FOR ENOUGH

"Elizabeth perfectly masters the art of getting it done. Stop analyzing, quit contemplating, and simply dive into Enough, a must-read for every entrepreneur or wantrepreneur."

— Chris J. Martinez, Founding Partner, The AutoMiner

"Every implementable lesson about entrepreneurship mastery I learned the hard way is laid out in this powerful and entertaining roadmap to finding massive success on your own terms."

— Julian Rosen, The Fearless Life Project

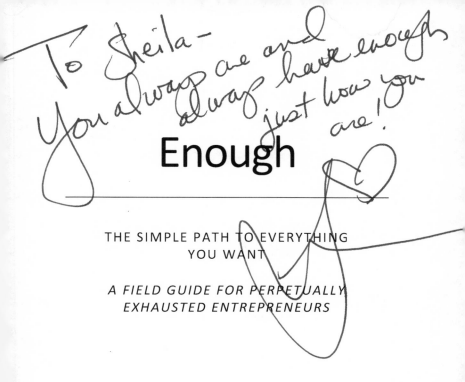

To Sheila —
You always are and
always have enough,
just how you
are!

Enough

THE SIMPLE PATH TO EVERYTHING
YOU WANT

*A FIELD GUIDE FOR PERPETUALLY
EXHAUSTED ENTREPRENEURS*

Elizabeth Lyons

FINN-PHYLLIS
PRESS

Enough / Elizabeth Lyons —1st ed.
ISBN 978-0-9998670-3-7

Book Cover Design by Sanja Stojkovic
Author Photography by Bridgette Marie Balmes

www.ElizabethLyons.com

Contents

For my beautifully adventurous kids. You have always been and will always be more enough *than I ever could have wished for.*

Also, for every person with whom I've ever felt enough as well as every person with whom I haven't. You have equal responsibility for where I am today, and I'm grateful.

FOREWORD

Have you ever felt the grip of life bringing you down, leaving you feeling stuck, frustrated, and on the verge of giving up? If you said No, you're not telling the truth. And if you said Yes, you're *exactly* where you need to be.

On the surface, it may seem like Elizabeth and I have very little in common. It would have been easy for her to see my message and assume she had *nothing* to learn from me. She says as much in the book: I don't carry the burden (or, *ahem*, pleasure) of endless carpools, practices, and dance recitals.

And yet, she did exactly what I've found people who are both successful and deeply fulfilled do: they lean in, and they sit in the front row of the classroom called life. They learn from anyone and everyone and drop their ego. In other words, she has a *growth* mindset: one where we understand there is always more to learn, we don't have all the answers...and we wouldn't want them anyway. We're here for the thrill, the chase, and the adventure of life. Learning, failing, and trying again are all part of it.

There's no better place to experience such adventure than in the world of entrepreneurship. However, in a world of do-these-seven-things-and-you'll-be-a-success, it's easy to feel lost. It's easy to feel like you have *too* many challenges. Or worse, that because your life doesn't match the highlight reel illusion of fist bumping and social media video clips, you're missing something. It's about you. You're simply not good enough.

And so, you dim your light or give up entirely. The tragedy in all of this, of course, is there are people out there waiting to hear from you. They want to learn from you. They want to hear your perspective and the value you bring to the world. Whether you have a brand, product, or service is irrelevant; they're buying *you.* But beyond all of this, *you* want to hear from you. Your growth in your business is all about cultivating belief, trust and, yes, love for yourself.

Enter *ENOUGH: The Simple Path to Everything You Want—A Field Guide for Perpetually Exhausted Entrepreneurs,* the book you're holding right now. You won't find a more honest, practical, and *real* world look at how you can navigate the beautiful (and sometimes murky) world of entrepreneurship. This is the handbook others claimed to be yet missed the mark. Their Hallmark card, picture-perfect accounts of life and business are things you and I can't relate to. Because they're simply not real.

The truth is: life and entrepreneurship are messy. But they're also riveting, fun, adventurous, and full of *is-this-*

really-happening moments that you wouldn't trade for anything in the world. And I'm convinced if follow even *half* of the advice in this book, you're going to achieve a level of success you've only dreamed of, while taking all the pressure off yourself. Win, win.

This book and Elizabeth's work serve as a refreshing, relatable, and empowering reminder that you are ENOUGH. Now dive in, and get ready to learn, laugh, and be equipped with a new perspective to create anything you want.

Tommy Baker
Resist Average Academy
October 2018
Scottsdale, AZ

WHAT IS ENOUGH?

"Belief in oneself and knowing who you are, I mean, that's the foundation for everything great."
—*Jay-Z*

PROLOGUE

"Do not let your fire go out, spark by irreplaceable spark in the hopeless swamps of the not-quite, the not-yet and the not-at-all. Do not let the hero in your soul perish in lonely frustration for the life you deserved and have never been able to reach. The world you desire can be won. It exists. It's real. It is possible. It's yours."
—*Ayn Rand, Atlas Shrugged*

There I was on a Saturday with the rest of the world crammed into Lululemon. I have a proven approach in that store. I make a beeline for the sale rack to assess whether or not anything demands to go home with me. I was in need of shirts, but I wasn't in love or even like with any of the available options. On to the yoga pants because...well...yoga pants. There were only two styles available in my size, one a patterned shade of eggplant and the other an olive green. And they were high-waisted. Solid gray and black are my colors when it comes to yoga pants, and I most definitely don't do high-waisted. Ever. But these bad boys were on sale. Big time. Now, I had at least six pairs of black and four pairs of gray yoga pants already at home in a drawer. Most of those were acquired on clearance at Old Navy for $6 because who passes up $6 yoga pants? I mostly liked maybe half of them, and I rotated through them the way my children rotate through the contents of the pantry. But they were practically *giving* these away. So while I didn't necessarily *need* another pair, was I really going to walk away from Lululemon yoga pants at 80 percent off? Even if they were high-waisted? I could probably just fold them over.

And then it happened.

I had one of those moments that isn't really about the moment at all—it's simply the moment's unfortunate destiny to be the occurrence that puts someone over the edge on which they've been teetering for quite some time. No. Just no. I had enough yoga pants. And you know what else? I'd had enough of a whole lot of other things as well having been running ragged as an author, jewelry designer, leather maker, coach, consultant, product inventor, project manager, editor, and mom of five for the past decade and a half. I had enough yoga pants. I'd had enough of being told what I should be doing (or thinking, or saying). I had enough not-yet-done items on the to-do list to last me the next two decades. What I didn't have enough of was peace. Or contentment. Or the sense that who I was—right there in that moment around all those other people who were practically taking each other down over 80-percent-off yoga pants—was or would ever be enough given the incredible amount of work I'd put in over the years.

I've been building businesses and inventing products based on my passion for fixing things and solving dilemmas for as long as I can remember. I swear that with each new venture I've embarked upon and each new problem I've vowed to solve—whether in my teens or my forties—it's felt like I was encroaching upon a brand new world wherein I had to, with record speed, assess the market, the competition, the newest ad fad, and the latest coffee craze that would get me from idea to enough, whatever the hell that was.

What *didn't* change throughout those decades of entrepreneurial adventure was the feeling that I was constantly running as fast as possible the wrong way on a moving walkway. Or, driving on the highway with both the gas and brake pedals simultaneously pushed to the floor. To quote the queen from *Alice in Wonderland*, "It takes all the running you can do to keep in the same place. If you want to get somewhere else, you must run at least twice as fast as that!"

Yeah, that wasn't physically possible. Not even for Usain Bolt.

And so I had to do something that was, up until that point, completely unheard of in my world. I had to stop. I had to look around. I had to acknowledge some truths that were extraordinarily difficult to acknowledge, even privately. And then I had to make the biggest pivot yet in order to permanently turn myself around and start walking the proper direction on the moving walkway like a normal person. And, because I both have known and know so many other entrepreneurs and entrepreneurial people who have found themselves in this exact same moment (even if it didn't come to a head in Lululemon), I thought, "That's my next book." I wanted to share the journey of going from *When I Am* to *I Am* and do my best to show you how you can do the same.

Before we dive into the following pages of admissions, strategies, revelations, tactics, and permission to treat yo' self whenever you damn well feel like it, let me make something abundantly and inarguably clear: You already *have* and you already *are* enough right where you stand (or sit, or with any luck, lie). You simply are. You are exactly where you need to be. This place may not be your intended ultimate destination, but that's another matter entirely. We never get to a point—not in this lifetime anyway—of, "It's enough. I'm finished. No more growing available to me here." But knowing that you already *are* enough and already *have* enough right this very minute is a critical place from which to begin this journey. We'll grow from here.

As a problem solver, mom of many and still-generally-trying-to-figure-it-all-out human being, there are statements—mantras, if you will—that I utter on the daily.

One of them is "You cannot be serious" (which happens to be the title of my third book). Another is "I'm sorry, what?" Or, perhaps you've heard me flatly say, "What the hell..." or "Meanwhile..." or "It's fine. Everything's fine..."

My latest favorite, as you can likely guess by this point, is "Enough."

To be sure, many times when I say "Enough" it's with regard to the antics of one or more of my children who, by route of some sick and twisted universal joke, are nothing alike. For example, when I believed that I'd finally found a comprehensive solution to a toddler's refusal to sleep in PJs unless they had purple on them, I was given a kid who didn't want to wear PJs at all. Ever. Unless we were on our way to a gala. And by "gala," I mean movie. Because when you're a mom with young kids and you don't get out much, going to the movies is often equally as exciting as going to a gala.

I recently posted the following question on Facebook: "What does *enough* look and feel like to you?" The answers were surprising, mostly because people's instinctive interpretation of the question had to do with having *had* enough. Comments such as "No more," "Enough means stop!" and "Time for a change" came flooding in. It hadn't occurred to me that I needed to clarify the variation of "enough" about which I was asking, but then again, when I ask people what they're reading right now, they respond, "This post." So clearly the onus is on me to be clearer overall! The word *enough* can be interpreted in multiple ways, but we tend to automatically trend toward the more negative one. I believe that the solution to that is choosing and thereby ultimately becoming the alternative, more positive, definition.

I'm assuming that, if you're reading this, you too are bone tired of running like mad to reach that ultimate destination where you feel like you have and are enough. You're also likely done with the trap of crap you continue to be consumed by between "I'm going to make this work" and the moment when you can profess, "Holy shit, that actually worked!" Don't even get me started on the moment when it actually does work and you wonder, "Why am I not more excited?"

I guarantee that we're not so different, you and I. The realities that cause us to lose our shit may differ; the number of shoes in our closet that makes us feel as though we have enough footwear may differ (I can almost guarantee that you have more, regardless of your gender); the sensation that reminds us that we are enough exactly as we are, where we are, may differ. But that knowing is what we're both searching for. And as entrepreneurs in a go-go-go-get-get-get world, we need a modicum of proven process to get us there before we reach the age of ninety-seven, when we'll be expressing our frustration to everyone in the old folks' home, where our fellow residents will be entirely unwilling—if not unable—to care.

It took that dramatic "holy shit" moment in Lululemon combined with a purposefully reset baseline of personal humility to acknowledge that my own greatest barrier to enough had never been the lack of a genuinely great idea, a shortage of friends or fans, or the absolute ability to realize my vision before I was too old to enjoy it. My greatest barriers were: one, getting endlessly stuck in the spin cycle between startup and growth, and two, myself. I was the walking definition of a person who needed to look in the mirror in order to get out of her own way.

When I was in a far less-focused point in my career (if you could have even credibly call it a career at that point), I had five ventures going at once. Doesn't that sound glamorous? It wasn't. I spent some days working on my jewelry business, some days on my apparel/homegoods lines, some days on leather goods, some days on book writing, some days on coaching, and some days on *Ohmigod I have the coolest idea for a new line of something-or-others I know positively nothing about for a niche market I know positively nothing about that has to be marketed in a specific way I know positively nothing about so let's get a clever domain name figured out by bedtime.*

I built websites and email lists and Facebook pages and Twitter accounts and YouTube channels and Instagram accounts, and I had visions of corporate retreats and glorious office spaces and loyal, driven, creative employees for all of them.

Meanwhile (told you I say that), my news feed was bursting with tragedy after tragedy, my Facebook feed was bursting with argument after argument over personal opinions about said tragedies, my kids would not stop putting empty granola bar boxes in the pantry and then getting upset with me when they didn't have granola bars to pack for lunch, it had been 120+ degrees out for twenty-three days in a row, and I'd spent half an hour of my morning debating whether or not I should purchase yoga pants that were in colors I don't care for and a style that is not even remotely flattering on me simply because they were 80 percent off.

The truth of that moment was, I didn't necessarily yet *have* enough, but I'd most assuredly *had* enough. From an outside perspective, everything about my life looked close to perfect (whatever the hell that is). But, behind closed doors I was thoroughly exhausted, running all day long yet crashing into bed only two steps ahead of where I started, if not one step behind. There was always more to be gotten. More money to make. More products to invent. More Starbucks to drive through. More social media platforms to figure out. More must-read books launching. More math homework I hadn't the slightest idea how to help a kid with. More behavior to analyze. More, more, more.

I was falling apart on the inside and had been for quite some time. The line from Anais Nin's poem that had resonated with me for so many years was suddenly screaming at me:

And the day came when the risk to remain tight in a bud was more painful than the risk it took to blossom.

I wondered how anyone gets to a point of calmly, gratefully, and quietly saying with conviction, "Enough already," knowing she (or he) both has it and is it. But that immediately became my new, number one goal. While I knew I'd continue to dream what some might deem a highly unrealistic scenario wherein I'd board a private jet every Friday afternoon with a covert CIA operative and we'd spend the weekend luxuriating at a spa somewhere by the ocean while my Great Dane casually lounged by my side, I recognized right there next to the Lululemon sale rack that, until that day presents itself (and even when it does), I needed to be clear on what it would take to be able to authentically say, "I have enough. I am enough" and be at peace regardless of the fact that everyone else was proclaiming, "But you could do and be and have so very much more!"

Each chapter of this book is based on a phrase or concept I've had enough *of* and have had to get rid of in order to reach my own downright heavenly place of *enough*. Perhaps ironically, this book wasn't written in hindsight, as many books of this sort are. It was written while I was in the midst of figuring this all out. It's about declaring that I've *had* enough of certain approaches when it comes to raising a family, building a business, and nurturing a network, and I've learned to accept and work *with* the non-negotiable aspects of building the business and life of my dreams while confidently staying inside what I know to be the boundaries of my unique purpose (and temperament). If we focus on the non-negotiable phases of our journey-slash-adventure-slash-horror-story-slash-triumph as entrepreneurs and honestly identify in which phase we reside at any point in time, we can more competently, efficiently, and sanely bust through to the finish line, unimaginably floored by what we've accomplished (and surprisingly unfazed by what anyone else thinks one way or another).

I finally took the time to identify my own unique path to *enough* in a way that has remarkably changed my life—not just my business life but also my life with my kids, my friends, my family, and random people I talk to for an hour in Starbucks who start out as perfect strangers and end up on vacation with me six months later.

Enough with the introduction already. May you also identify in the core of your being what your own *enough* looks like. May you know when to shout that you've had it and what to do afterward so that you don't end up in jail for verbally assaulting the bird that did an unexpected flyby in the parking lot, causing you to drop your coffee, shriek *What the Hell,* and start yelling at the bird at the top of your lungs. And, for the love of God, I've said it before but it bears saying again: may you know that through the entire process, *you already are enough!*

Let us begin...

GETTING TO ENOUGH

"If you're brave enough to say Goodbye,
life will reward you with a new Hello."
—*Paulo Coelho*

ONE

It's So Simple; Just Do It!

"Simple, not easy. There's a difference"
—*Ron Jeffries*

This book's subtitle is *The Simple Path to Everything You Want.* Because I know how enticing the word "simple" is, it's important for me to note right from the jump that simple does not mean easy. Simple and easy are two entirely different concepts.

I've engaged in no fewer than eighty-nine full-ass and 129 quarter-ass business planning sessions over the last few years. During these sessions, I sit with a friend and we talk about how fun it would be to do thus-and-such. We talk about exactly what the venture would look like, how many accessories or side products we might create, where we'd get an office, and who we'd hire. We look up distributors and supplies, research and register a domain name (or six) and look at the competition. All over four grande Holiday Soy Flat Whites. We get so excited. We're doing this. It's happening.

And then...nothing.

Because the reality of the *what* is so much more fun than that of the *how*. The *how* is where the details lie. The *how* is where we have to actually quantify the 89,674 steps we will take...just to enter the marketplace. Execution isn't sexy—not until you fall in love with the process of execution, anyway. It's easy to fall in love with the dream. Who doesn't fall in love with a dream? It's almost as easy to fall in love with the *why* behind the dream. But executing the arduous, perplexing, no-guarantee-included steps toward that dream? Staying up late figuring shit out and wondering if you've lost your mind through it all? That's not sexy.

Until you decide that it is.

Once you begin to have a sense of what *enough* looks like in your world, the journey quickly gets interesting. And by interesting, I mean over. Done. Caput. In short, the *how* of getting to enough is where most dreams of having and being it die a quick and relatively painless death (on account of it being so quick).

The shift from "When I am..." to "I am..." is definitely simple. But it certainly isn't easy. Remember when you were a kid (or an adult) and the first person in your circle figured out how to solve a Rubik's Cube? Once they discovered the trick, you could scramble that cube up like an egg and the person could easily solve it again and again. What they often didn't let slip was that they'd been working on cracking the code every single day for eight months, five days, three hours, and forty-two minutes before they solved it the very first time.

The Rubik's Cube obviously came out before game apps or Minecraft or Fortnite, but the analogy holds true. It's easy to become frustrated when you embark on an overwhelming adventure and someone all-knowingly professes, "It's easy! Just do it!" It doesn't feel easy. I mean, it's clearly simple, but the implementation of it isn't easy.

Every great why needs a great how

I may or may not have first heard the above quote in a Nicorette commercial, but you can't deny that it's spot-on. Processes are simple in the sense that there are clear steps. Navigating a fishing boat from California to Japan is simple. You get in the boat, point it in the right direction and sail. But it's not easy. There are storms to weather, sharks to avoid, worry to be had over whether you've lost your mind (you have), plans for delays, unanticipated emergencies, feelings of loneliness, annoyance with whomever you're with, etc.

When I hear people say, "I can give you my simple fifteen-step plan to becoming a billionaire," I hear what they're saying—and they aren't lying. They can absolutely lay out a fifteen-step plan to become a billionaire. The problem is that their clients will not, merely by employing that plan, become billionaires. Because each of the steps in the "simple plan" comes with emotional, financial, mental, and lifestyle-based hurdles and roadblocks that may or may not have been experienced by the expert who's providing the steps to begin with.

I feel badly for participants and coaches alike who find themselves in a scenario wherein they've invested in the fifteen steps to becoming a billionaire. Step One often requires that you do some serious work for four to six months to build a targeted email list, and that's when a participant says, "Yeah, you said this was simple. But it isn't easy. I don't have the time for or interest in this. I'd like my money back, please." In recent months, I've seen the more integrity-filled coaches (think, David Siteman Garland, Russ Ruffino, Mark Dawson, Amy Porterfield, and Nick Stephenson) get much clearer about the fact that, while they'll give you the steps—saving you an enormous amount of time, energy, and money—you *will* have to put in work.

TRUTH BOMB

I, Elizabeth Lyons, don't presently have enough in my personal, professional, and spiritual life solely because I'm passionate about what I'm creating. I have enough because I figured out the what, the why, and the how. I have faith in that which I can't yet see. And I execute like a motherfucker.

Within my own business, I provide clients with a clear, step-by-step plan for writing, publishing, and launching their first book as well as the coaching that holds them accountable and keeps them going week after week. In several cases, I co-author the book. The process I employ works time and time again. What's *not* the same time and time again are the lifestyles and mindsets of my clients. Sometimes people simply cannot hit the proverbial *Publish* button because they're terrified of criticism, and so we have to work through that. Sometimes clients don't believe that their stories are as valuable as their tips, so we have to work through that. Sometimes clients have incredibly moving, impactful stories that they don't know how to put into words, so we have to work through that. Sometimes clients can't decide on a cover design to save themselves and we have to get to the root of what that's really about, right after I do some deep breathing. It's not always *easy*, but it's always *simple*. The steps remain the same, even if it takes you a bit longer financially or emotionally to get through them.

Sometimes I compare courses and programs to a bonafide recovery program. Alcoholics Anonymous, for example, is known for having twelve steps. Those steps are simple. You go through them one at a time. Some take longer than others. But they aren't *easy* by any stretch, and anyone who's gone through the program will confirm that fact. Some steps take a few days; some take a few months (or longer). It's one thing to say, "It's time to make amends." The statement and corresponding concept are simple. But intentionally carving out the time to do the emotional work required to properly and productively make those amends is not *easy*.

In the area of coaching, courses and workshops, experts tout their accomplishments landing on the *New York Times* bestseller list with no prior writing experience, going from living in an alley to having six homes in three countries, or recently acquiring the opportunity to speak in Fiji every third Wednesday—all as a result of selling products they never touch through Amazon, growing a massive email list in thirty days, or learning to speak four languages in a month.

The reality is that the majority of them are undoubtedly telling the truth (or so I like to believe because the idea that people are knowingly conning others makes me reach for the high-calorie ice cream). And, in these check-out-how-far-I've-come sales pitches, they do an amazing job of selling potential clients on the dream that they've achieved. But, what they often aren't being nearly as transparent about is the fact that achieving that dream will require that your work ethic be as strong as your ambition—if not stronger. The fact that they accomplished what they did is, in fact, proof that you likely can too. But many of those who enroll in their programs or courses sign up believing that if they simply implement a simple ten-step process beginning on Friday night, they'll be J.K. Rowling or Tony Robbins by 5:00 Monday morning. And when that doesn't happen, they get pissed. This is precisely why the FTC now requires course creators to note that "results aren't typical." Otherwise, purchasers could easily claim they were duped, want their money back, and start a landslide of lawsuits against truly decent, knowledgeable, hard-working coaches.

Buy the dream. I encourage that. Be passionate about it. But fall in love with the process that's required to get you to the final destination because you'll be involved with it for quite a while. Be clear on the goal posts you'll need to pass along the way. And make sure that every action you take on a daily and weekly basis is in alignment with your ultimate goal. In short, avoid the Nutella aisle, and when you find yourself in it (and you will) turn on your heel immediately.

Dreams and goals are partners. "A goal is simply a dream with a deadline," said Napoleon Hill. The process of becoming—or, in many cases, un-becoming—in order to reach a goal and thereby realize a dream is just that—a process. One can implement systems to help them stay on track and continue moving forward, but no one can guarantee that, in 7.4 days, you're going to have a booming business or a bestselling book or a mile-long waitlist of clients on your hands.

No one buys the process because the process requires work, and work isn't fun. That's why it's called "work." You buy *into* a dream. But after that dream has been laid out so clearly that you can feel yourself resting on the edge of the infinity pool in Bali, the experts stop talking and many consumers begin sprinting fast and furiously toward absolutely nothing.

"Believe you can and you're halfway there"
-*Theodore Roosevelt*

This is an inspiring quote. And it's a true statement. But the fact is, believing will only get you so far. Without strategic, intentional execution, you'll believe for an entire lifetime but will likely never live out your dreams in real life.

I've been asked about the percentage of belief one must have in order to start executing. I'm sure it's different for everyone. But for me, it's hard to be at 100 percent belief all the time. We all have moments of doubt. We all have *moments* of zero percent confidence because confidence is a state of being, not a personality trait. We therefore also have *moments* of this-is-100-percent-happening confidence.

Here's my rule: you must work to feel at least 50 percent confident 80 percent of the time. You have to be strategically executing at least 80 percent of the time. It's not about working sixteen hours a day for the sake of working sixteen hours a day. It's about intentionally and efficiently executing in a way that works with *your* lifestyle and goals. If you work only four hours per day, make sure that 80 percent of that time is undistracted and intentional.

Even after you "make it" (meaning that sales have sustained themselves for a month or three), you can never lose your love of the overall process. Because there will, undoubtedly, come a tough month. Clients will flake. Unexpected bills will arrive. Mindset issues will start to creep back in. It's simply the life of the entrepreneur! I see it all the time these days on social media—one minute someone is celebrating his first five-figure month and the next he's posting that he feels like a fraud, needs to work on himself and is reconsidering the entire venture for one reason or another. *This roller coaster is totally normal!* The minute you think, "I have it made in the shade," the universe will remind you that it's in charge, and you need to sit yourself down and express some gratitude.

* * *

I have an incredible friend named Mike Young. Mike and I met a couple of years ago in a Facebook group. Truth be told, I almost never went into this members-only group. It terrified and overwhelmed me. It's a big group, and every time I went into it, there were a minimum of fifty-eight new posts by people in all different phases of Amy Porterfield's Webinars that Convert course—and they were all seemingly further along than I was.

The conversations in the group served as a continual reminder that I wasn't as far along as everyone else simply because I was dumb enough to be comparing myself to where everyone else was instead of comparing myself to where *I* was the day before, but that's another topic (which, of course, I'll get to). One day, I recognized that the only person I was hurting by continuing to attempt to figure out my particular challenge on my own was myself.

So I took a deep breath, entered the lair of all things webinars that convert, and posted my question. Within just a few minutes, Mike responded. Could it really be that easy? Yes and no. Mike's answer was spot-on, making what I needed to do simple but, of course, definitely not easy. It did, however, put me onto the correct obstacle course instead of leaving me to my own (inept) devices to figure out which obstacle course to engage with.

Mike and I became fast friends. He's a driven, well-studied, passionate visual brand and brand strategy expert, and as it turned out, the one thing he was spinning *his* wheels on was writing content. We quickly determined that I could write in about an hour what it would take him eight hours to put together. Because I learned long ago that it's critical to know your lane and stay the hell in it, I recognized that Mike and I could be of great benefit to one another. He understands the psychology of successful visual branding, and I understand writing.

I'd love to be cliché and say, "The rest is history," but I won't because the rest is important.

Over the next couple of years, Mike and I watched each other build our respective businesses. We celebrated our holy-crap-I'm-awesome-dude days and sent each other funny memes on days when one of us had texted the other, "Dude, what the hell... I seriously don't know what I'm doing right now."

It's always easier to look back on a situation or a span of time once the result has been attained. The "bad" moments seem so much brighter somehow. There was a day I clearly remember, about a month before Mike's business took off—you know, "overnight."

While driving through the foothills of Tucson, I returned the call he made to me earlier in the day. I hadn't received it because I left my phone in the car by accident, and upon realizing this, decided to go phone-free for a few hours. (The truth is that the parking garage was a long walk from my hotel room, and I didn't feel like making the trek.)

"So sorry, bud," I said. "I know we had a call earlier, but my phone was in my car."

"Hey bud," he said. "I don't think we had a call earlier actually."

Oh good. So I just apologized for missing the call that was never scheduled. Sounds about right.

He proceeded to tell me that he was just calling to remind me about hiccups and surprises. The day before, he'd had one of those moments where he thought, "Why isn't this working? Have I completed deluded myself into thinking this is going to go anywhere?"

And then that morning, he woke up with the biggest financial opportunity he'd ever had (at that time, anyway)—doing something he would gladly do for fun if he weren't getting paid for it.

"So just remember, kid, every single morning you wake up, remind yourself, 'This could be the day it all comes together.'"

Ever since, that's what I say to myself the moment I wake up, right after I list out everything for which I'm grateful, right before the kids start screaming at each other over who gets the last gluten-free frozen waffle.

The reasons each of my businesses over the years hasn't been as successful as I initially hoped differ. The common denominator, however, is me. In most cases, I listened way too hard to those who said, "This is going to go gangbusters." I believed them. And I simply waited. Because that approach is both simple *and* easy.

The key word in the above-mentioned quote from Roosevelt is "halfway." When was the last time anything completed only halfway had you jumping up and down like a lunatic? You will sit idly at that halfway mark forever if you don't tack some intentional execution onto the end of it.

I recently heard an analogy from Sarah Goodman detailing a particularly harrowing water exercise she had to engage in as a Naval Academy student. She explained that there are three places you can be when you're swimming: the top (where you can breathe), the bottom (where you can use the solid footing beneath you to boost yourself toward the surface), and the middle.

The middle is hell.

You have to *execute* when you're in the middle in order to either get to the top or sink back to the bottom (where you can push yourself to the top). If you just sit there in the middle and either panic or talk about how great it's going to be when you get to the surface, you're going to run out of air and die before you ever experience it. Literally. Yet we do this all the time when growing businesses, figuratively speaking. Having the dream, buying into everyone else's belief in its potential and waiting is the same as shacking up in the middle depth of that swimming pool. Before long, you run out of air.

Identifying the *what* is the easiest part of the journey. Sitting and envisioning one's future goals, the way life looks and feels and tastes once they've been realized is fun. The Law of Attraction is incredibly attractive, but it does not work without action, which is, I do believe, why the word "attraction" is a combination of the words "attract" and "action."

I've had conversations with friends wherein we lamented (at length), "Making $100,000 isn't that hard. It's just not. Develop a $5,000 service and find twenty people who are interested in it." That point is absolutely true. The challenge is that we say, "It's not that hard. So I'll start another day." If it were truly easy, we'd all be doing it. Conceptually it isn't difficult, no. But the fact of the matter is, you have to put together a service that at least twenty people believe is worth $5,000. That's not something that's accomplished overnight or with any amount of ease.

The *how* requires both work and patience. It requires a willingness to pivot and endure frustration and moments where you question nearly everything you think you know about yourself. And it's therefore within this part of the journey that most people say, "Forget it" and quickly remind themselves that they aren't special and it was never going to work anyway, so it's better to get out sooner than later.

But you know what?

The *how* is also where dreams come to *life*! The *how* is where "simple but not easy" becomes fun! The *how* is where both we and our businesses grow beyond our wildest dreams. It's where possibilities are truly limitless. And that is *why* it's so important to fall in love with the process of *how* so that you are part of the group that exits this phase instead of being swallowed up by it.

TIME TO TAKE ACTION

JOURNAL ACTIVITY

- In the past year, what have you expected to be easy that's simple but not easy?
- How has the reality of simple versus easy caused you to procrastinate (or give up)?
- What are you willing to commit (or re-commit) to with a new understanding that "simple" and "easy" aren't the same?

TWO

Paralysis by Analysis

"Nothing is ever enough when what you are looking for
isn't what you really want."
—*Arianna Huffington*

For so many years as an entrepreneur, I was just clear
enough on where I was going to start running as fast
as I could, but I lacked any semblance of a solid
tactical plan for getting there before my leg muscles
atrophied. There were also the constant distractions

known as Instagram, Netflix, and the sound of my kids disagreeing over who left the jelly out. But through it all, I continued to believe, "I'm running really, really, really fast, so I'm going to get there. At some point. I think. Right?"

Not so much.

Issue Numero Uno: I was running with scissors. And by scissors, I mean a lack of solid clarity and relentless commitment. I convinced myself that I had both because that was the easiest way out of that mess. But when all was said and (not) done, I didn't. Simple as that. Also, anytime anyone said, "You should turn left, Liz!" I did. Because surely other people knew me better than I knew myself, right? Additionally, if left ended up being the wrong way to turn, I could simply and easily blame the person who told me to go in that direction. It got to the point where I wasn't even completely clear on what I was running toward some days, but by golly I knew what it would look and feel like when I got there. I had the visualization part of the process down pat. And it was beautiful.

For as long as my parents can remember, they've had a hard time keeping up with my desire for the next big thing. As I pivoted from activity to activity and interest to interest (after spending a whopping day or two pursuing any one of them), my dad would get so frustrated that he'd shuffle across the room, shaking his head and lamenting, "Nothing is ever enough for her." (Yes, I see the irony.) Meanwhile, my mom was already on the lookout for the next bright shiny object, one that might perhaps, hopefully, for-the-love-of-God-*please* hold my interest for more than thirty-eight seconds.

Combine my lack of focus with my penchant for following (most) rules, and my approach to life quickly gets confusing, even unto myself. When I was six, I'd stand on the curb in front of our house, simply looking around while deep in thought—probably about how I planned to announce my newest interest at dinner that evening. When I say I'd stand on the curb, I mean that I'd stand *right on the curb*. Not a few inches behind it. Right on it. My mom would be having a conversation with a neighbor who was uncomfortably twitching in fear that I'd simply dart into traffic at any moment or was waiting for the perfect moment to escape, never to be seen again. This person's nervousness was distracting to the conversation, and my mom would ultimately say, "It's okay. Liz knows not to leave that curb, and she won't. She simply won't." She had as much confidence in that fact as some dog owners have taking their dog for a walk off-leash, knowing it won't run.

Until the day I did.

Now, to be clear, I didn't leave that curb. Ever. That wasn't a rule I cared enough about breaking to break. It was also a rule that involved not only my personal safety but the natural desire to please my mother, who was standing *right there*. But don't worry, the years of rule-breaking weren't terribly far off, even though it probably won't surprise you by now to learn that I had clear rules (clear to me, not to anyone else) around which rules *could* justifiably be broken. One didn't simply break rules to break rules. Not in my world anyway. I was incomprehensibly strategic about it all.

While I've had many spectacular daydreams (usually involving a beach; at least three of my crazy, amazing kids; and a smart, thoughtful, coffee-obsessed, hilarious man who bears an unmistakable likeness to Adam Levine), my greatest dream—ever since the days of choosing whether to step or not to step off the curb—has been to begin and end every day with reverence and gratitude toward my own personal *enough*. I want to sink into my bed every single night—regardless of whether or not the day was a "success"—confident that I was one hundred percent myself in every moment, making my own choices regardless of whether the justification behind them was valid or rational. It's what I've been working toward all my life—even long before I knew it was what I was working toward or what it looked like on a daily basis or how in hell to get there. Also important: know myself well enough at every stage of the journey to recognize the signs that I've *had* enough so I can nurture myself before I tell someone I care about to shove it. I wasn't good at this last part for many decades. I'm hoping a global "I'm so very sorry" will suffice.

Admittedly, "sinking into bed every single night confident that I was one hundred percent myself in every moment" is a relatively vague description of a North Star in life. It sounds lovely and poetic, but let's be honest, while anything is *possible*, very little is happening without a solid plan.

I am not a planner.

When I lived in Chicago, I could always be counted on to be caught in a rainstorm because I didn't look at the weather forecast. My mom carries an umbrella with her everywhere and always has, so perhaps my refusal to do so was reflective of my more rebellious side. Ironically, I now have an umbrella in my backseat at all times, and I live in the desert. I don't have an in-case-of-emergency water supply, but dammit, I have an umbrella.

Anyway, in order for the big dream to have even a sliver of a chance of coming true, I realized shortly after that glorious Saturday perusing the sale rack in Lululemon that I was going to have to determine, once and for all, what enough truly looks and feels like—*for me*—so I could walk in alignment with it. I also had to accept that none of it would manifest on its own. I couldn't sit on my couch and visualize or *Om* or vision board it into existence. It would require work—conscious, intentional, focused, deliberate, sometimes-confusing-and-grueling work. While this may not sound like a *holy shit* moment in your world, you better believe it was in mine. Because it was the moment I realized that I'd been living someone else's dream, seeking validation and approval from everyone but myself, and didn't even *like* what I was doing all day every day in exchange for a paycheck.

We all have dreams. We also spend ridiculous amounts of time judging other people's dreams while not nearly enough further clarifying our own, and that's a topic I'll dive further into in a bit. Some people are living what they *thought* was their dream, and they're miserable because they didn't realize that they built the dream someone else had *for* them (or a replica of the dream someone else had for himself or herself). Some people are living the dreams they had three decades ago, but they haven't stopped running the wrong way on the moving walkway long enough to consider whether or not those dreams are still of any interest whatsoever in the here and now.

Once we have clarity on our professional and personal dreams at any point in time, we love to think we can merely visualize them right into reality—immediately, if not yesterday. We want the huge house (or eighteen of them in different countries) or the adorable bungalow; the English Mastiff named Ernie or the Chihuahua named Euripides; a new Tesla (preferably self-driving) or a red, convertible VW Beetle; a life partner with whom we continue to grow and feel at home, and who brings us coffee in bed each morning; holidays spent in the islands with our favorite family members and closest friends; a daily, perfectly fitting clothing delivery from the psychic stylists at Stitch Fix; and a personal chef the likes of Jason Sani preparing each of our meals, snacks, and (extremely healthy) delectable desserts.

The *what* is where dreams are defined. And they better be defined intentionally and thoroughly or you'll build your skyscraper on the wrong plot of land entirely.

My path to *what* didn't always make sense, and it most certainly required a degree of commitment and focus I'd never before given. But the result is this:

> As an author, I write books to help or entertain people. As a coach, I help entrepreneurs powerfully write, publish, and launch their first book so they can grow their brand, expand their impact, increase their influence, and leave a legacy. As a mom, I'm raising five unique human beings to know what their own North Star is, never doubt that they can reach it, and say Thank You when I buy them ice cream—even if it's the flavor they collectively didn't agree on.

Dreaming about a life in which you have and are enough is easy. But until we qualify what that actually *looks like* to each of us and take appropriate action, it can't become reality. And, to be honest, once we dig a few inches below the surface, it's often not what we initially think it is anyway. How often have you thought, "When thus-and-such happens, I'll be happy," and then thus-and-such came to pass, and you weren't happy (or at least not as happy as you thought you'd be). The moment feels quite anticlimactic because what we really needed in order to feel that we were or had enough is far deeper than the superficial "thing" we initially believed.

I promise, it's never about *When I have* _____ or *When I become* _____ or *When I meet* _____ I'll have and/or be enough. The minute you utter the word "when" in conjunction with your definition of enough, you're toast. Why? Because you're putting ownership of that goal outside of yourself. You're relying on the acquisition of something (or someone) in order to feel whole. We have to know (very specifically, no less) what the goal looks and feels like in order to reach it. And we have to know that we're already enough *while* we're in pursuit of it. Whether you set quarterly or annual or overall life goals doesn't matter. What matters is that you set a goal, execute and refuse to define whether or not you have or are enough based on whether (or when or precisely how) you reach it. You have to live like you already have it and are it while working toward the tangible evidence of its existence.

The first step is gaining clarity on what you're going for. There are three core areas in which most people consistently strive to have and be enough: professional, personal, and spiritual.

Professional goals are self-explanatory. What is your area of expertise? Who do you help? How much money do you make doing that? How does that *feel*? Your personal life is defined by your relationships with others: friends, family, life partner, nosy neighbors, co-workers, you get the gist. And your spiritual side is the relationship you have with yourself. I promise, no matter how fulfilling your professional and personal relationships are, without having a strong and fulfilling relationship with yourself, you'll only be able to go so far in the other areas. In fact, the strength of your relationship with yourself directly correlates with the strength of your professional and personal relationships. As you strengthen your relationship with yourself, the intensity with which your professional and personal relationships will also improve grows exponentially.

We tend to judge what others have and whether or not it's a good indicator of what *enough* should look like for ourselves based on how happy that person appears to be. The key word here is "appears." I have stories for days about people who appear to have enough money, self-confidence, friends, clients, and shoes. Yet when I've had an opportunity to probe deeper, I discover that they are borderline broke, have the self-confidence of a flea, have many acquaintances but no true friends, or are saying that clients are banging down their doors but, in fact, they spend most of their time wondering when clients are going to start banging down their doors.

Or, they actually have all that they appear to have. And they're miserable.

All that to say, never use your perception of someone else's happiness, success, or sense of *enough* as the barometer against which you measure your current or future perception of your own state.

Ask almost anyone what it means to have enough, and you'll hear a similar answer: a house, a car, a healthy family, happy kids, a decent amount of sunshine, a vacation once a year, a job you enjoy at least 47 percent of the time, no stressful bills, good relationships. Then ask those same people if they have those things. When they say, "Yes!" notice the slightly confused look that immediately takes over their face. Why? Because they've just claimed to have all the things they need to have in order to believe they have and are enough. But they don't believe it. And the reason is, they haven't dug deep enough into the "things" they truly need, what they represent, and how to acquire or create them. What they want isn't the things themselves. They want the feeling that they believe comes with those things, except they based their notion that the feeling would come with those things specifically because it's what they were conditioned to believe, or it's what they've always assumed. They haven't gone deep enough into the correlation between acquisition and feeling to know what actually elicits the feeling of satisfaction that they're after.

People say, "I want the respect and admiration of others," and "I want to be valued," but those are both realities over which none of us has full control, so having our sense of self-worth depend upon them is dangerous. As someone who spent the majority of her first four decades defining her worth based upon what other people thought of her (or at least what she *thought* they thought of her), I can tell you unequivocally that said approach is extremely dangerous.

It's important to dive much deeper into the rabbit hole of each of the things you believe you need in order to have and feel that you are enough. You must determine what they represent at their core.

Understanding what something truly represents is critical to actually getting it.

I remember when my oldest daughter, who was away at her first year of college, was having a particularly challenging week. She'd been home the weekend before and was coming home the following weekend (she went to school two hours from home). She texted me on a Wednesday and asked, "Can I please come home this weekend?"

I reminded her that she was home the previous weekend and would be coming home the following week for a long weekend. I thought it best that she stay in Tucson for the weekend.

Beyond that, I inserted, unsolicited, "I don't think that 'coming home' is really what you're after. I think you want to escape."

"Uh, yeah," she responded.

Coming back home wasn't going to give her what she truly needed. You can leave the "scene of the crime" but the emotions stay with you. Plus, distracting yourself from the disappointment or frustration you're feeling won't make it go away; it will only take it on a little detour.

"What are you trying to escape?" I asked.

"Feeling crappy."

A relatively generic and yet common answer for any of us.

"Instead of looking at the upcoming weekend as an entire forty-eight-hour period of loneliness, frustration, anger, and general misery, take it one hour at a time and honor yourself from hour to hour," I suggested

"Yeah, all I want to do is...nothing."

"Then do nothing. Lie on your bed and stare at the ceiling until you think, 'I think I want to eat.' Then ask yourself what you want to eat and go get it or order it. Just keep following the road to what makes you feel good—as long as it's legal" (a caveat I feel I must always add when my children are involved to ensure I don't later hear, "You told me to do what made me feel good and this $450 hoodie or fifth of Jack Daniels did just that so the fact that I'm broke or calling you from jail is actually your fault.").

I get exhausted with ease. There's a lot going on at any one point in time in my world, and to be honest, that's not going to change anytime soon (if ever). I often find myself saying, "I just need a day away" or "I just need a vacation." But the truth of the matter is that I've tried that approach. I've taken a day or a weekend. And I come back Monday *not* feeling refreshed. Because I'm not clear about what I'm *really* seeking on those days or weekends away. It's not about lying in a hotel room bed for two days (though sometimes it is, and those two days are marvelous). It's about needing to get more in touch with myself. So I need to do things that are focused on that—not simply binge-watching Bravo—although there have been many a time when the antics of Fredrik Eklund, Ryan Serhant, and Steve Gold were all I needed to get through a challenging few hours.

Instead of wondering what million-dollar listing will be featured next, I need to read and hike and get a massage and eat healthy food and smile at strangers and hold doors open and notice gorgeous flowers and wear something other than PJs (but, let's be honest, it'll likely be yoga pants—just *classy* yoga pants).

One of the approaches that keeps people stuck is believing that figuring out what is enough for all of their life from today until the day they're no longer here is way too big of an undertaking. And they're right! The vastness of that answer is overwhelming because it's based on so many factors that may or may not become reality in the future, and it takes into account wildly different phases of a person's life (raising kids, working full-time, etc.)

The key lies in identifying what *enough* looks and feels like today and in the foreseeable future. And by foreseeable, I mean the next 100 days or so. Some people have a big five-year goal when it comes to work and personal life, but five years is a long time, and projecting that far in advance is overwhelming if you ask me. So they break that into more manageable one-year or even quarterly goals. Knowing what you need to accomplish in the next year in order to meet your own definition of *enough* can be broken down into specific goals. Many people identify between one and three major tasks they need to accomplish each week in order to move closer to their quarterly goal (after assessing what the one to three milestones are that they need to reach that quarter in order to meet their yearly goal). Then, when the next year rolls around, consciously reassess where you are and where you're going to make sure it still feels right.

Focus on the next 100 days. Identify what defines *enough* for you in that timeframe. Is your answer, "My business will reach the six-figure mark"? If you're not even at the five-figure mark, that's probably not the most plausible goal to set. Set a realistic yet slightly scary goal and be ready to put in place an execution plan that gets you one step closer each day. Be spectacularly clear about your goal. Is it to have a certain number of sales? A certain number of new clients? A certain monthly income? A dog that comes when he's called instead of bolting out the door when you open it a sliver to retrieve your latest Amazon delivery? What's most important is that you have an attainable goal, meet it (or don't and assess why), and move forward from there. You have to simply keep moving forward with intention.

Your goal must be measurable. It's not a strong plan to say, "I want to be happy" or "I want to feel loved." What does that entail? How do you measure whether or not that goal has been met?

Sometimes we don't want to really, truly explore what we want, and we procrastinate because we're afraid of something. In my experience, what we're oftentimes afraid of when it comes to our personal vision of *enough* is coming face-to-face with the current reality of our lives—and not being very happy with it.

Fear is an important emotion. Much has been written and stated in the past several decades about the joy found in being fearless, but in truth, fear is a critical emotion. If we fear nothing, we'll jump off of bridges and stand on top of moving cars and try to kiss rattlesnakes simply because it seems like a fun idea in the moment.

Such a heavy emphasis is placed on being fearless that I think people have misunderstood the point, which is that fear simply shows you where the boundaries of your comfort zone lie. Fear tells you what's foreign to you in one way or another. Fear shows you where you worry you might make a mistake. Are you afraid to pour cereal in the morning? Or start your car? Probably not. But I bet that before you'd ever started a car, the idea of doing so felt scary. Now it's just something you do 37,968 times a day.

Fear is an emotion to move toward. It's a signal that an opportunity for growth is near. Now, of course there are some areas where you should not move toward it, like the rattlesnake. But I'll trust that you're intuitive enough to know when fear is serving its intended purpose and when it's indicating an area of little-to-no comfort from which you can grow.

I remember a time when a friend of mine—I'll call her Samantha because I don't yet have a friend named Samantha—went to a spa for a few days. Those days were filled with massages and facials and reading and the kind of music that makes you want to take nap after nap, and she said it was heavenly.

One day she was scheduled for a treatment that suddenly didn't sound exciting to her, so she switched to a Reiki session. Different Reiki practitioners practice ... well

... differently, but her practitioner liked to say what was coming to her out loud, as long as it was okay for the participant. Samantha agreed.

The practitioner spoke various words that made sense—words that related to Samantha's life, activities she enjoys, and people she's close to. But suddenly a more out-of-the-ordinary word entered the mind of the practitioner. She reminded Samantha that she didn't know why she was becoming aware of any of these words or concepts, she was only communicating what she was sensing.

My friend prepared herself.

"The word I'm hearing," said the practitioner, "is vacuum."

As Samantha was telling me this story, I interjected, "Oh God, like you're always vacuuming?"

"No," she said quietly. "Unfortunately, I know exactly what it meant."

The interpretation was that her life was a vacuum. She spends all day every day doing all manner of "stuff," and she's very, *very* busy, but when she stepped back and looked at the value and the joy created from all of that stuff, she felt quite empty.

This is a horrible realization for many people. I see it a lot when moms of multiples exit the first three or four years of raising their twins or triplets (or more). They have been busy as hell for years feeding and changing and singing to and wrangling babies—so much so that they haven't spent much (if any) time on themselves. Suddenly, four years have gone by, and when I ask a question as simple as "What is your favorite color?" they either say, "I don't know" or "Blue." When I ask, "Why blue?" they respond, "I don't even know. That's just the answer I always give."

Or, they start bawling.

They realize that they've been super busy but feel as though they haven't really accomplished anything (in truth, they have, of course, done a lot of extremely important things; they've been keeping babies alive!). They've neglected themselves to the point that they don't even know their own favorite color. They haven't looked in the mirror (figuratively, and on many days, literally) in far too long.

This realization that one's life is a vacuum or that he or she is busy as hell but not really focused on or producing anything that's truly important can be jarring at best and depression-inducing at worst. But, if looked at the right way, it's an opportunity to shift. It's an opportunity to Begin Again. There is no reason that shift can't begin the very next morning (or five minutes later, for that matter).

We all know that person who never sits down. If and when they do sit down, will they feel as empty as I'm afraid they will? "Why" is a dreaded word when you're talking to someone between the ages of one and four, but outside of that realm, it's one of the most powerful. Whenever you're trying to decide if you are enough or have had enough, simply return to your *why*. What is the why behind a particular project or business idea? What is the *why* behind staying involved in senseless drama? I like to go six or seven layers deep into someone's *why*. It's never enough to simply say, "I want..." It's critical to get specific on the *why*. Beyond what you want, you have to know why you want it!

"I want to have $150,000 saved up so I can cover my daughter's college expenses without stress."

"I want to have $15,000 in my savings account so that I can comfortably take my family to Hawaii this summer for ten days."

"I want to earn $5,700 each month so I can pay my bills with ease."

"I want to earn an extra $100 this week so I can plant an organic garden in the backyard."

"I want to have two focused date nights each week with my partner so we can stay connected and make new memories."

"I want to enjoy thirty minutes of focused one-on-one time with each of my kids every week so they know they can talk to me about anything."

"I want to create a few hours to go shopping this week so I can have bras and underwear that actually match." (Don't judge, gentlemen. You know this is as high on your wish list as it is on ours.)

You have to clearly define your desires in your personal life. You also must define them in your professional life.

"I want to have 1,000 students enrolled in my course by end of year because that would allow me to quit my full-time job."

"I want to have 5,000 engaged Facebook followers by end of year because that would allow me to offer a course and have confidence in a successful launch."

"I want to enroll seven new clients in my high-ticket program by the end of this quarter because that will allow me to start the kitchen renovation."

"I want to have four calls with ideal new prospects booked each week because I historically convert one of every four, and my current capacity will allow me to enroll one new client per week."

Let's say you want to have 1,000 students enrolled in your course, what does 1,000 students represent? If your course costs $1,000, that would gross one million dollars in revenue. That would no doubt be wonderful and, I would think, allow you to quit your full-time job! But, if you are just starting out and presently have a list size of seven, is the enrollment of 1,000 students by end of year realistic? If so, based on what data?

Perhaps you work backwards (the term the cool kids are using is "reverse engineer") and say, "I want to earn $80,000 this year from this course because that will allow me to switch my focus full-time to this venture."

First, you have to know the *what*. Then the *why*. Then the *how*. One can't authentically exist without the other two. If it does, you'll end up in a situation where you get the *what* but aren't as happy with it as you thought you'd be, and because you have no idea how you got it you couldn't do it again even if you wanted to!

TIME TO TAKE ACTION

JOURNAL ACTIVITY

- What is it that you *really* want? First and foremost, what is the feeling you are after?
- Write down 10 words that describe the way you will *feel* when you achieve your ideal outcome.
- Now identify three activities you are passionate about. How can you execute on your passions in a way that will provide the ultimate feeling you seek? Identify three to five goals for the next 100 days that are in line with acquiring your ideal outcome.

THREE

Who the Hell Am I?

"You're writing your own book every single day. The problem is that you're not taking the time to read it."
—David Goggins

We have to be brutally honest with ourselves about who and where we really are at any one point in our journey. We create a mask based on who we've convinced ourselves the we are, who we think we should be, and who we think other people will like.

I recently had the most fascinating conversation with a client. We were talking about the difference between "act as if" and "believe as if." They're subtly—but critically—different. Acting as if, or assuming a reality that hasn't yet manifested into physical reality, works. But if we believe as if, we can get ourselves into trouble. Let me provide an example. If you *act as if* your business is successful and you're bringing in more ideal clients each week, loving your work and the value you're providing, you send that energy into the universe and it response (on its timeline) with the physical representation of that reality. If you *believe as if* your business is so successful that you have millions of dollars in the bank and a driver, you'll rack up a $750 bill at dinner, have your credit card declined, and endlessly stand outside on the curb waiting for a driver who isn't coming as well as a way to pay your bill (or pay down the credit card that was miraculously accepted).

There's nothing wrong with assuming that the life we dream about is already ours (because, on some level, it is), but we can do this while honoring our values. If racking up credit card debt and being stranded curbside aren't in line with our values, we don't have to put ourselves into situations wherein we behave as though they are. You can put on your nicest outfit and straighten your hair and put on mascara before you go to True Food for dinner because, as the successful, confident person you're assuming to be, that's how you carry yourself. But you don't have to hire a limo and buy a pair of Jimmy Choo heels to achieve the same level of assumption.

Part of getting honest with ourselves is being clear on what our lane is, what we are absolutely not good at, and what we flat-out don't do. I cannot tell you how freeing it is the first time you say, "I'm sorry, that's not what I do." (The word "anymore" may or may not be inserted at the end of this statement.) Especially when you've been saying "Yes" to doing it for all the wrong reasons and for far too long, publicly clarifying unto yourself and others the boundaries of what you offer is an incredible experience. For many years I wrote blogs, articles, and other such content for brands on a freelance basis. I didn't *hate* it, but...actually, I did. I hated it.

Doing that work reminded me of a story my aunt once told me. She's fluent in sign language and used to work as an interpreter. She had to behave much like a robot—whatever words the verbal person said she had to sign, and whatever words the deaf person signed she had to speak. This included derogatory remarks, terribly bad jokes, and outright bad information. That's exactly what I felt like when I was writing blogs and articles for brands. I had to write in their voice, so my own creative spin had to lie dormant while I produced what the client needed in the voice they needed it written in.

I remember the day I got a phone call from someone I truly enjoy working with. She asked me if I'd be available to write some blog articles for one of her clients. I thought about it for a nanosecond. It would be "easy money" that I could have used at the time. And, even if I wasn't in need of it myself, I could have donated it to a cause I support. But I knew that taking the time to write the pieces was time I wouldn't be spending in alignment with the pursuit of my personal *enough*. And so I said, "Thank you so much for offering me the opportunity, but I don't do that anymore."

Now, you might wonder why I don't enjoy writing blogs and articles for brands, but I deeply enjoy co-authoring books—books that must be written in the voice and style of the primary author. The answer to that is simple: I'm passionate about the stories of my clients. I'm passionate about telling their stories in their voice. To me, there's an art and a science to that, and I can get as lost in it as I do in writing my own books. Another subtle—but critical—difference.

I've spent a lot of time in life letting others be more aware of who I really am than I was. I've had moments where I've said, "Let's go out for drinks!" and friends have had to say, "Liz, you don't really drink." In most cases, they know that what I'm truly saying is, "Let's go out and catch up!" but why did I get into the habit of saying, "Let's have drinks?" I'll tell you why—because that's what everyone else was saying. Or, people have had to clarify what I'm innately good at because I wasn't confident enough in any given moment to own it (or aware enough to realize that innate talents are just that—innate. They don't require ten years of formal education or multiple commendations in order to exist, and we all have them).

Get real with yourself about who you are and where you are. You don't have to take out a billboard and let the world know, "I need a calculator to add 100 + 17." But until you are clear with yourself about what you are and aren't good at as well as what you do and don't enjoy doing, you have no compass by which to navigate whether the opportunities that come your way are in alignment with where you're trying to go.

TIME TO TAKE ACTION

JOURNAL ACTIVITY

This journaling activity is especially vulnerable for most of us. Please remember that you do not have to share it with anyone. You do not have to worry about being judged by anyone (and if you feel like you're judging yourself, stop it immediately). Powerful people are the most honest with themselves. They are the ones who cut all the bullshit from the journey and get to the ideal outcome sooner than later.

Start getting clear on who you are and where you are by thinking and writing about the following truths:

- I love to [insert activities]
- I absolutely detest [insert activities]
- If I had an entire day during which I got to do whatever I wanted and money was no object, I would [insert vivid description]
- I lose all track of time when I am [insert activity]
- My greatest fear is [come on, get honest]
- Complete the following sentences with as much content as comes to you: "What if..." and "But maybe..." Pay attention to whether your "what ifs" are related to things going really well or things not working. Pay attention to whether your "but maybes" are related to finding a silver lining or focusing on a potential negative outcome.

FOUR

Where the Hell is the Money?

"Remember that money will always match your mindset."
—*Joe Vitale*

It's time to get brave enough to say "Goodbye" to the old way of doing things. Because, put bluntly, if the old way were working, you would not be reading this book. If you do nothing else this week to move the needle toward your *enough*, get honest with yourself in the wee hours of the night with regard to your current starting point when it comes to your mindset around money (as in, the "for real" one).

To prime the pump, I'll share the reality of where my mindset was around money not all that long ago. I went through a large number of years wherein I sent a vibe into the universe that said, "Quite simply, universe, I don't believe that what I'm putting out there is worthy of cold hard cash in exchange." I wasn't forthright about that fact with myself or anyone else, and a slew of associated, buried limiting beliefs held me back. Badly. Part of the reason I held those beliefs was that I wasn't formally trained as anything that I was professionally offering: author, coach, or jewelry and leather designer. As a project manager, it was easier for me to step in and be paid to run projects because I believed that my experience working for a Big Five consulting firm provided me with a credible foundation for doing so. Also, that was a "real business," whereas writing and jewelry design were art, and coaching was just inspiring and motivating others, right?

Yeah, no.

I can't tell you the number of people who would look at a leather cuff I'd spent hours designing and making and say, "Oh, if only I could afford this." My response: "Just take it."

Those were some strong business skills, I know. I too shudder.

I struggled equally hard with the fact that none of my businesses took off in exactly the way I'd envisioned any of them taking off. My design business was the last one I managed right up until I went full bore into writing my own books and helping entrepreneurs write theirs full-time.

I remember the year I was trying to decide what to take up next. It was 2012, and I was between metal smithing and glass blowing. Would you believe (of course you would) that the deciding factor was the small matter that I could not put a furnace—a requisite piece of equipment for glass blowing—in my house?

Those were the two options I presented unto myself: put a furnace in my home or learn how to manipulate metal. I decided on the metal route and loved it from the first moment. I spent hours and hours teaching myself, and I sought out great teachers and the business didn't go even a little bit in the direction I thought it would, but it went in a great direction nonetheless. I learned to pivot, and the venture grew and likely could have continued to grow. There simply came a point where I realized that what I enjoyed so much as an art had become entirely too much about production. So now I simply do it as art when I feel the pull.

When I was in the thick of it, you can't even imagine how much research I did and how much money I spent identifying which designs would resonate with my audience instead of first getting clear on my own personal what, why, and how and taking an intentional step every day that was in line with that.

I was hell-bent on designing and making *art*, people. I spent hours and hours learning to solder silver without melting it, learning to etch copper with acid, and finding an unnatural and possibly suspicious level of satisfaction over watching a piece of rose gold heat to the point that it sunk perfectly onto a piece of silver as a beautiful orange flame bellowed up from below. These were the pieces I was excited to advertise and build entire lines around. And I positively could not get my head around the fact that the bestseller of all time was going to be a leather wrap bracelet that did not require a torch, an ounce of knowledge about fold-forming metal, or the studio full of incredible (and incredibly expensive) tools.

It made no sense to me. This leather wrap bracelet was something that I could teach one of my teenagers to help with if necessary. My teenagers who had *not* spent hours learning the ins and outs of flux and solder and torch angles. And so I resisted it. Heavily. The market was telling me flat-out what it wanted. But I wanted it to want something different. Because, the truth was, producing leather wrap bracelets day-in and day-out did not excite me. As a piece of art, they didn't have a unique story. And I could not make peace with the fact that people would gladly pay me more for that non-art than they would for a piece I'd spent five hours laboring over.

I wasn't making what I truly wanted to make all day, and I was having a hell of a time charging a reasonable amount for a product that was not only draining my very soul of life but that I didn't personally perceive as "art." I would say things like, "I can't charge that much for this bracelet; the materials only cost $8." Or, "Who am I to say, 'If you can't afford to buy this necklace that speaks to you, you don't deserve to enjoy it every day.'"

What I wasn't able to acknowledge was that 99.97 percent of the people I was saying this to or about *could* afford to buy my jewelry (and then some). They themselves were oftentimes in a scarcity mindset when it came to spending money. And allowing that mindset to be cast onto me created a vicious cycle of scarcity for both of us—and an inability for me to pay the electric bill without a panic attack! But hey, it was okay because I was of *value*. You know, to people I never saw again.

This is a place where creative people often get legitimately stuck. They create a business with incredible income potential, but it doesn't have incredible soul-satisfying potential. Those are hard decision points. Do you stick with the lucrative job that makes you start to lose an interest in getting out of bed each morning? Or do you make the incredibly irresponsible and impossible-to-understand choice and just give it all up? I didn't want to do either.

You've likely heard the parable of the flood. If not, let me regale you. A man was trapped in his home during a flood. He prayed for God to rescue him. His specific expectation in terms of the way this would go down was that God's hand would come down from the heavens, pick him up, and deliver him to dry land. His neighbor offered him a ride to safety, but he said, "No, I'm waiting for God to rescue me." Another group of neighbors came by in their boat and offered to throw him a rope and pull him to safety. He said, "No, I'm waiting for God to rescue me." Finally, a helicopter flew overhead and offered over a loudspeaker to send down a ladder for the man to climb to safety. He said, "No, I'm waiting for God to rescue me."

Ultimately, the man drowned. When he arrived in Heaven, he asked God why He did not save him. God responded, "I sent you a pick-up truck, a boat, and a helicopter. You refused all of them. What else could I do?"

When a business or venture of any sort doesn't grow the way you initially expect, you have to be able to have gratitude for and embrace the alternative, strategically pivot, or exit completely. Had my overall *why* been "be a well-known metal designer who focuses on custom, high-end work" I could (and would) have pushed through and found a way to pivot. But my *why* simply wasn't that strong when it came to jewelry and metal design as a business. In fact, the business aspect of it was eroding my passion for it altogether. What it was time to pivot toward was a business for which I was extraordinarily passionate when it came to both the creative *and* business aspects.

I also now recognize that, more important than it was for people to value my unique work, what I was really seeking was their value of *me*, and as much as we might like to think that one's value can be measured in dollars and cents, it cannot. I believed (albeit subconsciously) that if a piece I created benefitted someone's life, it was my spiritual duty *not* to charge them for it. After all, I might be providing the only happy moment in that person's day. I desperately wanted to be valuable. I wanted to take care of people. But I wasn't happy. Because my happiness was dependent upon being needed (and, therefore, valued) continuously. Which was dependent upon my producing product continuously. For which I wasn't making nearly enough money in most cases. It was exhausting.

Money is a loaded topic for a lot of people for a lot of reasons. Some people believe they are worth more than they are. Most people appear to believe they are worth less than they are (and not just in the area of money, either).

There's a direct correlation between self-worth and net worth, but not in a when-I-have-money-I'll-feel-good-about-myself kind of way. In fact, it's the exact opposite. One's self-worth affects, both directly and indirectly, one's net worth in so many ways. If your self-worth is low, not only will you not charge enough for your products or services, you likely won't be comfortable leaving the house long enough to let people know those products and services exist!

People with high self-worth actively seek opportunities to increase their net worth. What they don't seek are ways for others to increase their *self*-worth. It's not about over-charging or taking advantage of someone else. Ever. It's about knowing and showing through your actions that you know that your work is of value.

You have to be really clear about how your ideal customer derives value from your product or service. You can't see your product or service merely as a commodity that serves *you*. Many people have to create the time and intention to drastically change their relationship with money. I was unconditionally one of those people. We initially think that having a lot of money means that we're valuable and secure, but we don't believe in ourselves enough to charge what we're worth. So we're broke, and therefore, not valuable. And because we believe that we aren't valuable, we aren't comfortable appropriately charging for our products or services. Or, we work *too* hard to prove our value to others. We borderline beg people to purchase. Or, we say, "My process or product or service might work. It might not. Take it or leave it."

That's super inspiring.

You must find a healthy balance between believing in yourself and your product and having respect for the fact that everyone has to make his or her own decisions when it comes to how and on what to spend their money.

Recovering from this scenario and realigning your relationship with money is a process. It starts with making a vow that you will never again work for less than you believe you're worth. Another strategy I employ is "act as if." Even if you don't believe you have the credentials to sell your work for a specific amount of money, act as if you do. This slowly starts to retrain the brain. But this action goes beyond the idea of "fake it 'til you make it." Simply put, if you're faking it, the universe knows it. You have to believe it unequivocally. And then wear that confidence to the meeting, sales call, or networking opportunity. People sense a lack of confidence and disbelief from a mile away, and it's the sticking point that keeps them from shouting, "Hell yes, I'm in!"

Just after David and I decided to be partners-in-parenting instead of partners-in-life, I considered renting space at a co-working office downtown. Working from home was positively stifling, and I believed that a change of scenery would greatly help. At that time, any investment beyond that which was required to pay for the must-haves every month was not only scary, it was inarguably stupid. The rent on the space I had found was $350 per month, including parking, and it was the least expensive I could find for an office with a door that wasn't in a dungeon because, if I haven't yet mentioned, the quality of my environment greatly affects my productivity.

So $350 per month plus gas money plus, undoubtedly, some lunch purchases and coffee runs equaled *Ohmigod how dumb am I?* I tried talking myself out of this investment every which way. I honestly don't think anyone in my inner circle thought it was a particularly grand idea. But, in the end, I did it anyway. I cannot even fully tell you why. I somehow knew that I simply had to. That if I didn't, I wouldn't be able to build a self-sustaining business, and doing so was critically important to me.

I remember the day I moved in to the office space. It was on the seventh floor (thank God for elevators), and I furnished the entire office, from my desk built from steel pipe and wood to the massive frames I hung on the wall, hand-lettered with You've-Got-This motivational tidbits. I was only there for six months, but the relationships that were formed while I was there carried me through the next several years professionally. It's actually where I met my friend Kirk, who you'll hear more about later. His insights have been instrumental in getting me from where I was to where I am, and I'll be forever grateful. It's also where I met Vann and Shane (you'll hear about them again too).

In order to change the way you think about and interact with money, you have to first change the way you think about and interact with yourself. Ironically, the truth is that, at its core, this process is actually not about changing your relationship with money. It's about changing your relationship with *yourself*.

Women especially have a tendency to see themselves as caretakers. Flawed. Undeserving. Of lesser value. And those qualities can make it real hard to accept a big payday. Overcoming this obstacle requires deep spiritual growth. If I were to bet, I'd bet that if you're uncomfortable accepting money for your services, you're probably also uncomfortable accepting compliments or allowing someone else to do nice things for you.

While writing this book, I came across a book by Kate Northrup titled *Money—A Love Story: Untangle Your Financial Woes and Create the Life You Really Want*. I bought it immediately, had it wirelessly delivered to my iPad, and started reading. If you are closed off to self-love, you are also closed off to receiving value from others— and that includes financial value. You don't let people open doors for you, claiming to be a "strong, independent woman." You don't like to let other people treat you to coffee. You feel like, as a natural caretaker, you should be the one treating everyone else. You perhaps worry about why they want to treat you—do they think you are broke? Are you now indebted to another coffee date—one where you'll pick up the bill? Listen, if you can't see your own value, the world can't see it either. Nor will they give it to you. Expand your capacity to receive in all areas. Accept compliments graciously. Accept offers to provide you with value by covering the cost of your grande Holiday Soy Flat White. Accept help that others offer to provide.

Owning your value is a critical component of the structural foundation of *enough*. I didn't begin to flourish—not just financially but spiritually—until I put my focus on what I truly love and, dare I say, am really good at instead of what I mostly liked but also thought would make money combined with what looked really good from the outside but felt positively stifling. I simply felt lighter. One of my best friends, Erin, who's known me for almost a decade, said to me one day, "You're just different. Your energy is totally different. The fact that you're truly focused on living in alignment with your North Star is clear."

But it's been far from smooth sailing. There was a dire day in my world that occurred not long ago. I affectionally refer to it as Day 214. It wasn't August 2nd (the 214th day of the year), nor was it the day I drove 214 miles dropping off, picking up, dropping off, and then again picking up kids from school.

It was the day I received an alert on my phone that I had $2.14 in my checking account.

I just sat there staring at the notification as though through winning a staring contest with it I could move the decimal two places to the right. And add a zero to the end. I finally summoned the courage to login to my checking account to identify what was surely a mistake (and not on my part). Sure enough, my balance was $2.14, and I knew that, with a large number of monthly expenses being auto-debited from that account, I was also likely to go negative and begin racking up a series of insufficient funds charges.

The first thing I did was call Mike because, after all, he was my partner in this whole dude-what-the-hell-am-I-doing-wait-hold-the-phone-I'm-amazing adventure.

"Um, I think I've made a grave mistake," I started. "This is horrifying."

"What's going on?" he asked, genuinely concerned.

"I...I just got an alert. I have $2.14 in my checking account."

"Okay?" he responded, as though still waiting for me to reveal the details of the situation.

"That's it," I clarified. "Did you hear me? I have $2.14 in my checking account!"

"Is this the first time this has happened to you?" he asked.

Apparently, hitting rock bottom in one's checking account is a fairly common occurrence for entrepreneurs, and while I don't think it should be or has to be a rite of passage into this ridiculous world of ideal life creation, it certainly happens far more often than I was aware. Upon talking to two or three other members of my inner circle, all of whom are also entrepreneurs, it became clear that I was, indeed, the last member of that group to be inducted into this extremely prestigious and horrifying club.

The amount of shame I initially carried over the position I suddenly found myself in—before having any idea that this position was "normal"—is unfortunate. All of my credit cards were maxed out, so I no longer had those to fall back on, and even though my mailbox was receiving between three and eight pre-approval notifications for zero percent interest introductory rates on new credit lines each week, they'd all been declining my subsequent applications for months. This seems an extraordinary waste of ink, paper, and postage, by the way, but what do I know?

While I didn't want to ask anyone to help me in that moment, I'm extremely blessed to have people I *could* ask if I were at risk of losing my house or my car or my air conditioning in the middle of July in Phoenix. I also had some assets I could liquidate in order to free up a small amount of cash. I am aware that there are people who have *no one* to go to and *nothing* to liquidate in these moments, and they deserve some serious credit (no pun intended) in my opinion because I seriously don't know if I'd hold it together under those circumstances.

Mike told me, and I quote, "That sucks. I know it's a bad feeling. Take a few hours and feel bad about it, and then suck it up and get the fuck back to work."

And so I did.

I so badly wanted to make a few phone calls and create a patch by way of a short-term project management gig or writing assignment. For a few minutes, I kicked myself for having told my previous client, "I'm sorry, but I don't do that anymore." But I forced myself to sit down at my desk and write about book writing. I turned off (as best I could) any and all thoughts about scarcity and insufficient funds fees as well as ramen noodles and what sauces would best complement white rice, and I continued to remind myself why I was doing what I was doing.

Within four days, I'd secured an $8,000 contract. It didn't stop there. Over the next thirty-nine days, I secured $29,500 in contracts. The money wasn't yet in the bank, but the deals were done, and more than anything else, I was confident that, even if every single one of those clients cancelled on me, I could find new ones to take their place. They weren't a fluke. They were solid leads who came as a result of the trust, faith, and belief I had in the existence of a specific ideal outcome wherein I was providing specific value to a specific client that—until that point—simply hadn't yet manifested in my physical reality.

Here's the deal: Day 214 could very easily happen again. Once you come out of that scary financial place, you aren't permanently immune to it. Which is why your mindset around money simply *has* to change. Because money is energy, it requires the opportunity to flow. Stay aware of opportunities to give to others. I know that the phrase, "There's always someone who has it worse" is real tiring when you're already more exhausted then you've ever been, but it's true. We have homeless individuals on nearly every highway exit within thirty miles. I can't help every single one of them, but I have my "regulars." One of them has a sign that says, "Homeless but not hopeless." Even when the bank account had $2.14 in it, I gave him whatever change was in my car—because he was standing outside at the end of an exit ramp in the middle of the afternoon when it was 110 degrees out, and I wasn't.

Rich and wealthy are different concepts, not unlike simple and easy. In my world, being rich has to do with the balance in my bank account (which is somewhat absurd when you think about the fact that it's really nothing more than a ledger. Cold hard cash rarely touches my hands. I'm known as the "cashless wonder" because I almost literally never have it on my person, and bills higher than a twenty terrify me). Being wealthy, on the other hand, has to do with the balance in my soul. I choose to be wealthy at all times. I see my bills as an investment in my life, not a cost of living. After all, I chose my house and my car, to keep the thermostat at seventy-eight degrees, to eat as healthy as we can, to have Hulu and Netflix subscriptions, to go to the movies occasionally, and to go out to eat and laugh with friends.

But, in the area of one's bank account balance specifically, the difference between rich and not rich has no direct correlation with the difference between good person and bad person. There are plenty of millionaires who are outright assholes, and there are plenty of people looking through couch cushions every week in order to buy a gallon of milk who are driven, genuine, hard-working, kind people.

I talk to prospects all the time who have brilliant stories but they're afraid to be bold enough to publicly tell them. I ask, "Do you realize the irony here? The phenomenon holding you back is exactly what you want to help your readers push through? Energetically, *you* have to push through first. Otherwise, there's not authentic alignment."

This is often the point in our communication when their name goes onto my whiteboard as someone to stay in touch with while being well aware that they'll have to work through whatever is holding them back before we can work together. Or at least acknowledge its existence. Clients from this esteemed list have reconnected with me all on their own enough times that I now fully trust that part of the process. And, more importantly, I have to honor it when I'm guilty of the same energetic mismatch and take a day (or three) to work it through.

When you are someone who has spent his or her entire life instinctively having a dreadful reaction to upcoming expenses, your current bank account balance, or the unexpected expense popping up (and, so you're completely aware, I *am* that someone), it takes focused effort to train your brain to think differently. Whenever I spend money on something unexpected, I do my best to say, "There's more where that came from." I remind myself that money is just energy, and just as energy must flow, so must money. If I hold onto all of it with a vice grip, the universe will hold onto its share as well.

Quite simply, you are worth. Period. You already *are* worth. You don't have to earn your worth. You were born with it. Your job for the rest of your life is simply to believe it.

TIME TO TAKE ACTION

JOURNAL ACTIVITY

- What is your current, *genuine* financial position?
- Regardless of the answer, are you fulfilled day-to-day?
- What are your limiting beliefs when it comes to money?
- What are some words, phrases, or actions you need to intentionally remove from your vocabulary when it comes to money?
- How might the barriers between you and a steady stream of clients be mirroring internal work that *you* need to do?

FIVE

Bright Shiny Object!

"I was going to take over the world. But then I saw
something shiny."
—*Unknown*

I n my experience, Target is always a solid place to start an amazing adventure. So let's talk about what happens when you glide through those glorious red doors (a shade of red that is, for the record, trademarked and almost as securely behind lock and key as is the recipe for Bush's baked beans). You stop in for toothpaste and sandwich bags. I know it sounds absurd that you'd go to Target for only two things, so let me remind you that you were just there yesterday, at which point you spent $100.89 because it's certifiably impossible to get out of there for under $100. During yesterday's trip, however, you forgot that you needed toothpaste and sandwich bags, so you thought you'd pop in *real quick* on your way home to grab them.

On the way to the aisles that contain those items, you see a sale sign by the candles. Orchid & Lavender is now 75 percent off at $4.99, and you grab it because you might need a gift at some point to take to an impromptu gathering. You return to your trek to the toothpaste aisle. But hang on—you've spotted Nutella! You haven't had Nutella in so long. It's like heaven on a spoon, and you'll be the kids' (or dog's) hero for eight whole minutes if you bring it home as a surprise. Yes, I realize dogs perhaps can't have Nutella, and it's not something I'm feeding mine; everyone calm down. Anyway, you stop to grab a tub of it. At which point you notice that they're now combining peanut butter and jelly in a container. Like psychopaths. You take out your phone to text a photo of it to your best friend. *Can you even believe this shit?* You now have a candle and a jar of Nutella, and you're headed to toiletries for the toothpaste. But there's an end cap filled with As Seen On TV items. There's that slicer that cuts an onion into perfect squares without making you cry.

This goes on and on, and once you finally make it to the register, you're carrying nine things you don't need and you've lost forty-seven minutes for the second day in a row—but this time on an errand that only needed to take four. And you get home only to realize that, once again, you forgot toothpaste.

SHORTCUT TO ENOUGH

Have clarity around who you are, what you're going after, why you're going after it, and how you'll get it. Whenever you are distracted by anything that isn't in alignment with that goal, immediately stop yourself. and head back toward the toothpaste aisle.

As entrepreneurs, we often unknowingly take a similar path in our businesses, not to mention life in general. Replace the candle aisle with a new technology that can make your email process more efficient; the Nutella with a new, surefire social media posting strategy; the PB&J concoction with a drama-filled group of people who are both completely irrelevant to your business and provide zero personal value but definitely give you something fun to talk about (you know, to avoid working on the task that has you momentarily perplexed); and the As Seen On TV end cap with your feeling that, if only you'd gotten that miraculous teeth whitener, every person who ever dumped you would immediately call and profess how stupid they were.

In general, whether to float effortlessly downstream with thousands of people or fight to swim upstream with just a handful quickly becomes a conundrum not unlike the never-ending debate on which came first, the chicken or the egg. As analogies go, fewer people choose to swim upstream against the current, so it's a less congested space in which to operate. My question is, why are we spending so much time analyzing whether to swim up- or downstream? Neither is inherently right or wrong. The issue is that we don't pick one and commit!

We each have to decide in which direction we are most comfortable traveling and why. In my case, abrupt re-direction without a solid *why* or *how* in place only made life (much) harder. In truth, early on I chose to swim against the current simply because I was sick of people, and at that point in time, living with some degree of a masochistic mindset. It was not in any way a strategic, thought-through plan. I mean, for God's sake, if you're going to swim against the current, at least wear flippers and do some weight training ahead of time. On multiple occasions, I pushed and pushed and pushed only to lose my footing and find myself quickly whisked back downstream. Several of those times I'm pretty sure I waved at my original starting point as I flew right by it. There is a distinct difference between strategically thinking outside the box and tirelessly reinventing the wheel just to be different, and the latter is a complete waste of time.

In my case, I turned around and started floating downstream. Because if you're miserable going one way, the solution is obviously to do a 180 and go in the opposite direction, right?

Not so much.

Insert problem: I had no idea why I was now swimming downstream other than the fact that it was the exact opposite of what I'd always done. I knew I was doing something different, which felt foreign and scary and exciting all at the same time. But all of my energy went toward the acknowledgement that I was going in the opposite direction, which felt awfully strange and hard and I didn't want to drown. I didn't know why I had turned around. I didn't know what to expect. I had no plan, no raft, no sunblock. In almost every way, it was no different from swimming upstream except that it was less work from time to time.

At the start of the Christmas season just after I turned four, my parents got out the boxes of tree lights, and as is typically the case, they were twisted into a jumbled, knotted, multi-colored mess. I pulled out a huge ball of tangled lights and encouraged—with the worst lisp my parents had ever heard and in a way that was much more of a demanding *this is happening now* than an encouraging *is anyone interested?*—"Come on, guyth. Let'th get organithed!"

I then sat down and deeply focused on one and only one goal: untangling that ball of lights. I identified the goal, assessed the tools I needed to accomplish it, and went for it. I allowed no distractions—not the sounds of kids outside playing SPUD and freeze tag, not the awareness that *Mr. Rogers* was coming on soon, not the sudden desire for Spaghettios. Because, as Lisa Nichols so eloquently stated, "Convenience and conviction do not live on the same street." It was just me and the lights and the determination to get them untangled so we could wrap them around the Douglas Fir my dad sawed down with his own two hands (and a saw) that morning at our local tree farm.

That was likely the last time I strategically, intentionally, patiently executed toward a clear goal with intense (lasting) focus and determination for several decades. Go back to anyone's youth and, I swear, you can see the innate mindsets that will shape their entire life. I'm a psychologist's dream.

Within a year or so of the light-untangling venture, I invited my parents to play a game. Not Checkers. Not Go Fish. Not Candyland. This game had no name at first. But I knew the rules from the get-go. I explained to my parents how the game was played, and we got started. Ten or so minutes into the game, my parents became confused. It seemed the rules were changing. And they were. The way this game worked was, the rules morphed when necessary so that I was always winning and the game never ended.

At one point, one of my parents asked, "What is the name of this game?"

And I responded, without hesitation, "Jakbat."

Thus, over the years, anytime I concocted any sort of game, plan, or business idea, my parents would look at one another, smile, and say, "Oh God. It's Jakbat." Jakbat had become code for "Liz's imagination has been captured by a bright shiny object. She may focus on it for a year. She may focus on it for ten seconds. We'll just wait it out."

With any one of those ideas, instead of sitting down and methodically doing what needed to be done to reach a definitive end goal, I'd sit down with the proverbial Christmas tree lights, drop and break one, go to the kitchen for a broom, spy dust on the microwave, get a microfiber cloth to eradicate the dust, take the cloth to the laundry room, realize that no one had switched the wet laundry to the dryer, make the switch, stop into my daughter's room to see if she was caught up on *Gilmore Girls*, get on YouTube to research "best ways to untangle Christmas lights," get caught up in recommended videos on funnel hacking, think about how confusing a topic *that* is, contemplate the idea of writing a book that would *un*complicate it, decide what to title that book...you see where this is going, right? Never mind the fact that not long after being completely distracted from my original goal, I'd stand in the center of my kitchen and wonder, *What the hell was I doing again?*

Listen, the list of businesses and products I've conjured up is long. I swear I invented the self-warming ice scraper; the Sharper Image simply got to the patent office faster than I could (also, they knew what the patent office was. I was all, "Just make it by midnight and sell it everywhere by morning. How am I going to do that? Who knows. I just am." Very inspirational and ballsy, yet not an approach that *ever* works.)

When I was a freshman at *The* Ohio State University, I was one of the only students in our dorm with a word processor. Once word of this got out (pun intended), I began to be asked to type up other students' papers. By "other students," I mean an entire flock of sorority girls from New Jersey who were usually out until 2:00am, at which point they returned to the dorm slightly inebriated and very much panicked because they had a paper due six hours later.

My phone (the kind that's attached to the wall, with a cord) would ring in the middle of the night, and some panicked girl who could remember my phone number but not my name would beg, "Pleeeeeeeaaaaaaase can you help me?"

And so I did.

For one dollar per page (two if the call came in after 2:00am), I typed up and printed out these girls' papers. In the beginning, I'd call them when their papers were finished, and they'd come to pick them up. Or, out of the kindness of my heart I'd deliver them. But after one too many instances of no answer at the door or not having correct change, I switched up my policies. The new rule was: we agreed to the price up front, and I left the finished papers in front of their doors where they had left me an envelope of cash. It was as close as I ever plan to get to a drug deal, and it worked brilliantly.

Now, this was back in my people-pleasing days when I just wanted to be liked by everyone—sorority girls from New Jersey included—and so I was doing it more for that benefit than for the money. That is, until I realized that I didn't really care for these girls, therefore didn't care if they cared for me, and stopped answering my phone at 2:00am. I also realized I could make more money (and save a whole lot of sanity plus my coveted sleeping hours) working at the Law School Library. So I said, "Enough of this," and retired from Sorority Sister Support. Someone else picked up where I left off. She's probably running a billion-dollar company somewhere right this very minute, not caring much whether or not anyone likes her.

Between my sophomore and junior years in college, I applied for, and received, an opportunity to work abroad in Japan. My degree of study was Japanese. I absolutely loved it, and I had zero ideas about what I was going to do with it. Anyone beginning to see a pattern here? My professor, Uchida Sensei, thought the opportunity would be perfect for me, so naturally, I went for it. Because someone else told me I should.

Long story short, I ended up in Tokyo a few months later as an intern with the one participating company that was on Year One of its participation. It was a renowned candy factory (hello), and on Day One it became clear that my job was going to be standing on the assembly line ensuring that my koala bear cookies were belly-side up before they went through the machine for an injection of chocolate into their bellies.

Given that fortitude wasn't yet my strong suit, I determined before the end of Day One that I was outta there. I spent the first two hours sitting in the common office space at a desk from the 1950s with executives on either side of me explaining (in Japanese) the corporate structure of their company. I can still see in my mind's eye the diagram they pulled out. I kid you not, it looked like an extremely complicated architectural rendering. In the event that I need to clarify, it was *written* in Japanese. There was literally not enough Advil on the planet, and I took to simply saying *Hai* (yes) every eight seconds or so. And then, when I was instructed (in Japanese) to put on what looked like a Hazmat suit to go stand by myself (I mean, unless you count the thousands of koala cookies as good company) by that assembly line for the next six hours, my new objective became undeniably clear: get the hell out of there.

I wish I'd been able to treat the opportunity as an adventure, find the positives, find all the reasons to laugh about my predicament. But that's not who I was at that time in my life. When I was determined, I was determined. But I was often determined in not-so-productive areas that involved much more drama than personal growth. It was what it was.

Getting out of there was no easy feat. I had to find pay phones and racked up an $800 long-distance bill over the next four days calling my parents and coordinating my return from this hellish nightmare that I couldn't see an alternate solution for or find a silver lining in if you paid me in chocolate-filled koala cookies and sushi for days.

Once back in the States, I decided I'd start a consulting firm to help other wayward study-abroad students navigate their expat adventure. I remember it like it was this morning. I setup my office in my loft and wrote Goldstone Communications (Goldstone is my maiden name) on a piece of paper and slipped it into the front of a three-ring binder. By mid-morning I was completely overwhelmed by the thought of what to do next, and the venture ceased to exist.

My first year out of college, my roommate and I (both working ridiculous hours for a consulting firm) often got home from work at a completely unthinkable hour and made S'mores. One night, we got the idea to pen a gourmet S'mores cookbook. Can you really blame us for wanting a legitimate (and write-off-able) excuse to continue making S'mores every single night? Didn't think so. We sat there for a few hours, came up with all different ways to make gourmet S'mores, named them, named the book (for the life of me I can't remember the title, but surely it was creative), and imagined our book front and center at Williams-Sonoma (along with S'mores samples, of course). Self-publishing didn't yet exist, the "how" of getting this book created or proposed to a publishing house made us eat more S'mores than was healthy, and by the wee hours of the morning we decided we were better at eating them than telling other people how to eat them.

Shortly thereafter, when I was newly married, I got the idea for a petit four company called Petit Four Your Thoughts. Is that not the most brilliant brand name you've ever heard? I thought so too. My then-husband bought me a petit four baking kit from Martha Stewart, and let's just say that my first batch did not turn out real well. The frosting definitely did not flow onto those cute little cakes the way one would expect or the way it did when Martha made them. It more *plopped* onto the cakes. In clumps. It was not appetizing to look at or ingest.

That big idea was quickly doused by two things: a strong resistance—or rather, an outright refusal—to honing my craft at petit four making, and all the people (and by "all", I mean three or four) who said no one would spend money on such a small cake. That made some amount of sense because no one had yet done it. But when $3.75 cupcakes from Sprinkles hit the big time several years later, I was like, "I have *got* to stop listening to other people (and persevere a bit more in the perfection of my skills)!"

"Do you not remember my petit four idea?" I'd say to everyone in my inner circle? They didn't. "But what a cute concept! I bet that would have done really well!" Right. Unfortunately, the idea, while clearly brilliant, didn't last long enough for anyone *to* remember it before I was off and obsessed with another idea.

There are about eight-seven similar stories where these came from, but you get the point. Focus wasn't my thing. Because fear and a lack of self-discipline owned me.

* * *

I recently took my first trip to Napa, California. I wasn't there for more than seven minutes before I wondered why I'd never gone before, and I'm (still) not much of a wine drinker. One morning, having gotten coffee (which we purchased at a caboose-turned-cafe I could've died over), my beautiful friend Natalie and I were walking back to the house we were staying in when I saw the most perfectly formed, bright orange California Poppy growing out of a crack in a driveway.

I've long been fascinated by plants that grow where, by all accounts, they should not. Entire bushes that grow from the tiny creases and crevices between rocks in areas where rain is infrequent; weeds that grow like wildfire even when you starve them of water, half-decent soil, and sunlight; poppies that bloom in all their glory out of the dirt-less cracks in a driveway, just spreading their petals and saying, "Don't you tell me I can't grow here." All the while, all the organic dirt, water, and kind words in the universe can't keep an aloe plant alive around here, but who knows what that's really about.

The poppy could not care less that it's not supposed to grow there. It spends no time listening to its friends—the roses and chrysanthemums and tulips—who continue to tell her she's crazy. She simply focuses on her North Star, her ideal outcome: growing in *this* crack on *this* driveway. And the greatest part of it is that she's actually more glorious than her friends, who are planted where they think they *should* be. She conserves her energy and is consumed not with what anyone else thinks but instead with what *she* wants.

I'm sure that, at some point, the flower had to wonder, "Should I try to bloom over there next to the rose garden?" And, yes, I'm aware I'm taking this flower illustration a little too far. But you get it, right?

As humans, we have an innate fear of "letting things go." We wonder, "But...what if this is *the* 'big idea?' What if I'm so close and I just let it drop?" Let me make this very simple for you: there is no one Perfect Big Idea. There are many *great* ideas, any of which can portend great success—but only if you truly focus on the process that will get you there! So get real clear on exactly what you want to do, and eliminate all other distractions.

As I mentioned earlier, for years I split my time between five very different ventures, thinking, "Whichever one launches first is the one to which I'll give my full commitment." I finally recognized that if I only gave 20 percent of my effort to five different ventures, I'd only get a 20 percent return (at most) on any one of them. If you're ready and willing to invest 100 percent of your time, only then can you hope to get a 100 percent return.

During that time period living as a mildly schizophrenic entrepreneur, when people asked me, "What do you do?" my answer was often, "How long do you have?" Or "On which day of the week?" For a while, that made me feel very vogue, very accomplished. But multi-tasking is a myth, and I would argue that none of us does it terribly well.

I tried an infinite number of approaches: focusing on my product line on Monday, my writing on Tuesday, my design business on Wednesday, coaching on Thursday. But, inevitably, something came up for jewelry on Monday—perhaps I'd get a series of orders I wasn't expecting—and it would take me completely off course. I had whiplash trying to go back and forth from one effort to another because they were so wildly different. My audiences were different, my messaging was different, my strategies were different. I had no clear brand identity, even unto myself. I loved each venture, but not devoting myself to just one of them was exhausting. I think this is how the Bachelorette must feel when she's down to "three amazing men." You can't have a strong, life-long relationship with three amazing men (I mean, some people supposedly can, but it's confusing). You have to choose ONE. It's not even that one of them is destined to work and the others aren't. Once you're down to three compatible people, it comes to choosing one and giving your all to that relationship. So it is with a business venture.

Think of it this way: for only one business, you have a client base to build and maintain, a website, social media accounts, leadmagnets, sales pages, and an email list (for starters). Managing all of those assets is unconditionally a full-time job, and the idea that you can apply a great degree of care to more than one of those at a time (especially if you are a one-man or one-woman operation) is nothing short of asinine. You're hoping that one of them will take off, and then that's the one you'll give your full attention to, but you're preventing *all* of them from taking off because you're not giving any one of them all of your attention. The universe isn't really sure what to give you, so it gives you (at most) a 20 percent return in each area. You're spinning your wheels, shifting course like crazy, and wondering how to pay the water bill with your very vogue, very busy career.

In 2011, I invented a product called the Hold It Baby On-the-Go Toy Organizer. It was brilliant—am I allowed to say that?—and it deserved to sell far and wide to all the corners of the world, ensuring that no child ever again said, "Uh oh" after dropping his sippy cup or board book or Matchbox car or can't-live-without-blanket from his car seat, stroller, or high chair.

Sidenote: the parent company of the Hold It Baby was named Jakbat. I'm a full-circle girl, if nothing else.

The reasons it didn't do better, if I'm being brutally honest, had to do (almost) completely with me. When the product was in the launch phase, identifying the over-arching dream was, of course, easy. My dad (who is a super-smart engineer and was my business partner) and I would release this incredible product to wide acclaim, then develop several accessories, then design a variety of super fun patterns, then expand deeper into the market, then have an incredible warehouse-style facility where our employees loved to come to work every day, with lunches catered (by Jason Sani, of course), motivational retreats (led by Tommy Baker, of course), and weekends filled with trips and adventures with family and friends or by ourselves when we were absolutely positively sick of everyone.

Our early days were filled with discussion over— among other topics we didn't realize were utterly irrelevant to our ultimate success or lack thereof—

whether or not we should patent the initial product. The argument for doing so was, "If we don't, a big company will steal the idea and all of our customers." It was a valid notion, and of course that might have happened. Just look at Crocs or Beats or fidget spinners or jelly for God's sake. Everyone's copying everyone because the idea that someone else has done the hard work of figuring out what consumers want and now all that's left to be done is putting it out there and making millions of dollars is compelling. But, at the end of the day, what *cannot* be copied is a solid brand and the brand loyalty that follows. If a new company is able to make a better product less expensively *and* provide more amazing service to customers than the current leader in the space, they deserve to acquire those customers. But, that doesn't happen as often as you might think.

The fact is, most companies or writers or service providers don't have to worry about someone stealing their product idea, book plot, or service concept because what's *actually* required to make it successful is *far* more substantial than the idea itself. And this is the point at which most people fall short. They want the dream, but they don't want to work the process required to get there. They want consumer loyalty, but they don't want to do the work required to create a unique brand that attracts (and keeps) its ideal customers.

There are enough customers in this world for every single product and service—as long as we are each authentically doing what we do. Think about it: we all have something unique to offer that will attract the perfect client or customer. Therefore, trying to be like someone else in order to grab their client base is a waste of time because it's neither genuine nor sustainable. One day we'll have to admit that we aren't that peppy all the time, our "kids" have four legs not two (even though we've invented a product "for parents by parents"), we don't really like to swear, or we can't teach someone how to be brave through tandem skydiving because it's something we ourselves we would never—and I do mean never—do. I make it a rule not to speak about or coach in any area that I haven't experienced myself more than once or twice. Which is why neither tandem skydiving nor snake handling will ever be recommended activities for my clients.

Back to the Hold It Baby, more than worrying over whether someone was going to steal our concept, our energy should have gone into how we were going to corner the market and provide such incredible service than no competitor would matter. Our focus wasn't powerful enough. Our marketing strategies weren't honed enough. Our budget wasn't strategic enough. Our expectations based on the enthusiasm of friends and family weren't realistic enough. Our endurance wasn't strong enough. We had bills to pay, and so on we went to the next dream. Looking back, we may legitimately have been one tweak away from a Hold It Baby world takeover, but instead, I have 506 of them in my garage. Everyone I know with a baby now knows what they're getting for Christmas this year.

What was the *one missing piece*? It wasn't a patent. Or a celebrity spokesperson. Or a solid understanding of Facebook ads. It was consistent, focused, intentional execution toward a clear goal.

I remember a conversation I had one day with my friend, Kirk. He works incredibly hard and grows more successful by the year. He also drives me insane because he works "slowly." I think that, in strategic circles, it would be said that he works "methodically." But to me, it's just slow. There's too much analysis given to seemingly insignificant details and far too much time spent focusing on "little" tasks.

I'll tell you a story that might effectively illustrate this, even though it has nothing to do with business. He and I are both DIYers. Sometimes, when he has a new project to undertake, knowing that I love that sort of thing, he'll ask me if I want to build whatever it is with him.

One Sunday, he asked me to help him build a small entertainment center.

When I walked into his house, he had his laptop on the kitchen counter with five open Firefox tabs, each displaying directions for a different entertainment center. In my mind, there was far too much analysis already going on. Just pick one. (This, for the record, is an approach I do not plan to change. Paralysis by analysis is very real, and it's wildly unnecessary. Pick something. Pick anything. *Just pick!*)

After seven minutes of him justifying why this one versus that one might make more sense, I said, "I can't do this. Pick one so we can get to building it already."

And he did.

It was then time for a trip to Home Depot. Thankfully, the entertainment center design he chose came with a list of required supplies and wood cuts. Of course, however, he wanted to modify a small portion of the unit.

Were it my project, here's how it would have gone down: write down the top ten items on the supply list, go get them, believe the whole project cost only the $87 that the first trip to Home Depot cost, go home and get started, and realize nine minutes in that I couldn't complete Step Two without the fifteenth item on the list. I'd then drive back to Home Depot. This time I'd only spend $8. Not expensive at all.

This exercise would go on and on until I had all the materials I needed, had returned or ruined beyond the point of no return those I did not need, screwed boards together three times instead of one (no time to read directions here), and spent $18 on each of twenty-seven trips, making me think the project wasn't terribly expensive but too tired to do the math. When someone asked, "How much did that cost?" my answer would be, "Only about $45!" when the reality was more like $397. They'd be kinda pissed when they went to buy all the supplies in one trip, like a normal person, and got to the register. Please note that I well approximate that timeline and hit Decline on the inevitable incoming phone call every single time. It's a valuable skill.

During our planning session (the one I deemed wildly unnecessary) there was a lot of, "So if I take this end off, I don't need this piece of wood, but if I add a shelf here, I'm going to need two extra 2 x 6s, and these plans call for 1 x 6s, but I don't want those so I have to make everything 2 x 6s."

Throughout this endeavor, I'm pretty sure I impatiently stared out the kitchen window, tapping my foot and doing something analogous to the loudest *Ujjayi* breathing on record.

Seven hours later (it really did seem to take that long), we headed to Home Depot. The grand total was *not* $87. It was more like $195, and the trip took forever. But the thing is, we didn't have to go back. It took an hour to unload the car and sort everything out, but then the project came together like clockwork.

At any rate, this "methodical/slow" approach makes me crazy, yes. But I can't argue with the fact that, in business anyway, it allows him to steadily grow with clear data to analyze every quarter while I sit over here like a crazed maniac, moving from to-do to to-do, having little-to-no idea what's working, what isn't working, or what the hell to do about it.

Fast forward a few months. Kirk and I were engaged in an entirely different (and more business-focused) discussion. I'd like for you to think of someone in your life who could say to you, "Those pants do not look great on you," and instead of yelling, "F*ck off!" you'd respond with, "Oh. Ok. Thanks for telling me" because you know that person genuinely wants you to look and feel your best and, having zero to do with her own personal interests, she knows you do not look the way you want to look in those pants.

This was one of those moments. I know Kirk wants the best for me (when we aren't strategizing a DIY build), and I therefore knew that his words held no intention other than helping me. But they were still not easy to hear.

He quietly said, "I'm seriously concerned that you're going to find yourself in a 'situation' sooner than later." Smart man that he is, he tread lightly, knowing that one verbiage misstep is often cause for me to see red, him see me see red, and him begin running in the opposite direction, discussion over.

"What kind of a situation?" I inquired. "Does it involve a beach and a Great Dane?"

"No. Unless you're living in a tent on the beach with a stray Great Dane."

There were ten to fifteen seconds of silence during which he was probably praying for his life, and I was praying to keep my mouth shut because all I wanted to do was yell, "EXCUSE ME? You think that little of me? You think I'd allow myself to end up in that situation? You think I don't have hustle? EVERYONE thinks I have hustle! EVERYONE!"

Instead, I simply said, "Oh. Um, ok?"

Sensing it was safe to go on, he continued.

"You always land on your feet, yes. You figure a way out of every situation. There's no denying that. But I'm always wondering, 'What's the plan?' You spend 20 percent of your time on each of your five *very* different ventures. You spent all day yesterday starting a sixth. Do you really know when you're going to take a leap in any one of them? And, is there a plan that says you can jump from higher up each time with greater confidence that you'll land on your feet? Or are you going to keep living by a prayer that when you want to jump, you will, and hopefully it'll end up okay."

In case you're wondering about that sixth venture, the week prior Erin and I got a great idea to go Live on Facebook and do a bit of a *Seinfeld* thing talking about nothing yet everything and it went kind of okay. Seriously, we had nine or ten viewers at one point, and I don't even think any of them were robots. So we decided to turn it into a show called...wait for it...*Meanwhile*. By mid-day, I'd created us a Facebook page, a YouTube channel, and an email account, and I was researching the best domain name (because, obviously, Meanwhile.com was claimed years ago, and while it was available for purchase, the asking price was $150,000). So now I had *six* ventures on my plate, each of which would get approximately 16.66 percent of my time. Definitely not heading in the right direction.

Back to my conversation with Kirk. I was still quiet, and the blood wasn't obviously rushing to my face, so he continued. "Businesses have five phases: Idea, Start up,

Growth, Expansion, and Maturity." (As you might imagine, this was when my eyes started to glaze over. I felt like I was back in a college lecture hall.) "You have no problem with the Idea phase. Or the Start Up phase. But you get stuck in growth. You're impatient. And the minute a new idea pops up, you're on to that—*especially* if someone else tells you you're good at it or it will do well. Any one of your ideas has had great potential and could have gotten to the Growth phase, but you have a philosophy of jump and grow wings on the way down. Which I get. But if you have a choice of five cliffs to jump off of, you just pick one and jump. I, on the other hand, want more a bit more information about all of my options."

I so wanted to be angry. Offended. Insulted.

But I couldn't.

Because he was right.

I wasn't focused. I wasn't intentional. I wasn't clear about my worth or my value. I was afraid of failure, and I was afraid of success. So I stayed uncomfortably between the two.

One of the reasons I had such a hard time committing to just one venture was that I honestly had too many limiting beliefs, most of them related to what I was capable of. Therefore, I relied too much on others' beliefs and opinions about what I could and should be doing. I hoped that others would show me the way by partnering with me to create something sustainable. I relied on others to show me which venture was my true calling instead of declaring it for myself and then making it so, come hell or high water.

I loved saying, "I have five kids and two businesses," but the truth was that I couldn't really call any of them a business in the true sense of the word because none of them was reliably bringing in more than $500 per month (and a couple of them were costing me money every month). But it was okay because it was all going to launch soon. I could just "feel it."

The conversation with Kirk forced me to absorb and make peace with the reality of my situation. Or, perhaps it didn't force me after all. Perhaps I was simply ready to hear the truth that I'm sure others have attempted to put in front of me many times before, the truth that Kirk swears he's attempted to put in front of me many times before. I don't remember any of them.

You have to know not only what value you provide but also to whom you provide it. Even when I finally made the decision to choose the one of my five ventures about which I was most passionate, my coach told me I had to niche down one more level.

"Not possible," I responded. Famous last words.

Within ninety days, I'd niched down not just one more level but two. And my business was growing more quickly than ever. Imagine that—a far more narrowly defined service available to a far more narrowly defined audience than ever before, and not only was it was flourishing, I was completely in love with my job to the point that I didn't think of it as a job. The positive ramifications of this affected not only me.

My twin sons, Jack and Henry, are sixteen years old. They could not be more different from one another. Jack is a naturally gifted athlete and problem-solver, and Henry is a naturally gifted artist and comedian. Three out of four of those are not inherited traits—not from their maternal side anyway.

Both have been saying for some time that they need to get a job. Jack's schedule doesn't really allow for it since he has sports practice each day until after dinner. He has the car that he and Henry share, so Henry's left without transportation to get to/from a job. One day, it occurred to me that Henry spends hours—sometimes six or seven at a time—illustrating. The kid loves it. He ultimately wants to work for Pixar. Time flies for him when he's drawing. Jack, on the other hand, is the business guy. He's the process guy, the marketing guy. So I said, "Just a thought. What makes you guys think you have to get a job a Starbucks or Target or, God help me, Taco Bell?" I suggested that Henry sell the illustrations he works so hard on, and Jack immediately chimed in, "I'll be your manager."

Exactly what I was thinking.

They then proceeded to "pull a Liz," as we say, and forecast how they'd handle it when commission requests, opportunities to appear on *Ellen*, and invitations to collaborate with Kanye started pouring in, but I quickly brought them back to Step One: list a drawing somewhere and see if it sells. And so, the Etsy exploration session commenced.

Every time Henry began to dive too deep into thoughts such as, "Maybe I could do spray paint art," or "I'm going to need entirely better canvases for all of this," I reminded him that he was already spending six hours (that felt like one) drawing. Start there. That's where your passion is. Find that market. Grow that tribe. Expand from there. We'll see how this goes. Stay tuned.

Laser focus in terms of what you do, who your client is, what you don't do, and what you charge is non-negotiable. If it doesn't scare the crap out of you the first time you assess what you do and who your client is, your focus is quite possibly not honed enough. A friend of mine recently joked that you could narrow your market to men in Phoenix, ages thirty-four through thirty-six. with beards, who like to skateboard, only wear yellow Converse, make at least $125,000 per year, and list "sloth" as favorite animal, and be scared to death thinking that—if you're lucky—there's *one* of these individuals in existence. But you'd likely be pleasantly surprised to learn that there are sixteen of them, and if you provide great value at a price point of $7,500, you have the potential to gross $120,000 per year in Phoenix alone. Narrowing your offering and your market can feel limiting, but it actually makes client acquisition far more efficient and your value proposition far more attractive. Who do you help, or who does your product help? What do you or your product help them with? How will they benefit from working with you or using your product? Get focused on the answer, and then put your feet in (figurative) concrete and start executing.

* * *

Once upon a time, I woke up with a great idea. That night I went to bed with an altogether different—but equally great—idea. Doesn't that sound consistent and promising?

It wasn't.

The dream I woke up with was to start the petit four company, and the one I went to bed with was to run a massive petit four/books/apparel/candy empire. I'm the queen of a process I affectionately refer to as "And then I will..."

It goes something like this: I'm going to start Petit Four Your Thoughts out of my kitchen. And then I will rent an amazing space downtown with brick walls and an open ceiling and vintage crystal chandeliers. Then, I will expand and also sell great books and hilarious socks and maybe even muffin tops and eclairs. And then I will open a second shop. And then I'll be asked to bake my petit fours live on *The Today Show*. And Kathie Lee will wear her cuff that day and I'll be all, "Ohmigod I recognize that!" and we'll have a laugh. And then I'll custom cater a fancy Hollywood party. And then I'll have my own show.

And then I remember: I don't even know how to bake an edible petit four.

One thing I do really well is dream. Perhaps this is why, at my core, I'm a storyteller. It's easy to dream your way toward an amazing result, and it happens in various areas. With some level of frequency, I'll see an ad for a new workout program. Everyone on TV looks so happy doing it. They're sweating a lot, but it's almost as though they are glowing. And their smiles combined with their grace while doing those lunges. It looks almost...fun! And all the testimonials! Man. If that woman with eight kids and 120 pounds to lose can do it with a smile, then by golly, so can I.

If you think my dream stops there, you're wrong. When, after just twelve weeks, I'm in the best shape of my entire life, I'll purchase the bikini I've been dreaming about for years and book a week-long trip to the Maldives (that I can't afford—presently) with the picture-perfect romantic partner (that I don't have—presently) and I'll get those amazing pants from Lululemon that I'll look and feel amazing in and wear them on the plane in my first-class seat (which I also can't afford—presently) and I'll somehow maintain that physique through daily juicing with the juicer (that I don't own—presently) and it's going to be perfection.

But first, I have to order this set of workout DVDs, and I'm too tired to stand up to grab my wallet. So I'm going to need a new plan.

I remember talking to a friend who runs a non-profit. He said to me, "One month at our board meeting, someone suggested, 'We're going to raise $40,000 this year.' And I thought, 'That sounds great, and last year I would have jumped on board, but last year we only raised $6,000, so how about we figure out how to raise $10,000 this year and go from there.'"

And then I promptly thought, *Holy Shit*. Because earlier that day, I was on the phone with someone talking about my membership program and that, before long, it would generate $37,000 per month. And my friend said, "Wow! That's amazing! How much is it generating per month now?"

$185.

Then there was a pause. "So," she cautiously began, "how do you get from $185 to $37,000?"

At the time, my answer was, "One person at a time."

Which is true. But going from $185 per month to $37,000 per month is an arguably huge leap. So perhaps a more effective plan is to work toward $500 or $750 per month, see what's working, and then scale up instead of looking at the grand goal but having no plan to get there.

One morning I lied in bed and thought, "If I can sell 1,000 copies of *Holy Sh*t...I'm Having Twins!* per month, I bet at least 200 of those people would buy an Elizabeth Lyons Design T-shirt made especially for moms of twins. And of those people, I bet seventy-five would buy a coffee mug. Before I got out of bed, I had an entire coffee mug line designed (in my head) but no plan to get 1,000 women to purchase the book every month, which was the requisite top of that funnel!

Dreams are amazing. Focus is critical.

Believe me, I know it can feel slow. I know that studying the data and analyzing trends and split testing and taking things a single step at a time and watching ads run for ten days without changing a thing in order to get enough data to make a logical decision is painful as hell. I feel like I'm bleeding money right out of my veins every time I do it. And yet I'm so thankful that I've learned to take this approach.

When you have a business that does really well every August, but you have no idea why, you have no idea how to build upon it (and extend it to other months as well). When you have a piece of jewelry that sells better than another and you don't want to work with it because, to you, it's the least "artistic" piece you sell, you're forcing on the market what the market doesn't want. That's not a business; that's a hobby.

I know this, of course, because it's happened to me. When I became obsessed with making jewelry, I was intent on learning everything I could. I sought out the best teachers (hello, Dara), I rented studio space, I saved up for the best tools. I practiced and practiced and practiced. I made some real crap for a while, let me tell ya, but I kept going because I loved making pieces and I loved who I got to spend time with while I was doing it.

Your life is undoubtedly quite full—in terms of the amount of "stuff" you have going on. I know mine is. And you know what I had to get really honest with myself about? Parts of my days were full of *not* moving forward! They were full of complaining about where I was, of wondering why I wasn't somewhere else, of working on projects that were peripheral, of spending time with people and on things because I believed I *should* but I sure as heck didn't want to. They were full of being sucked dry by other people's drama because, one, it gave me something to do that gave me a worthy justification not to focus on work and, two, if I wasn't providing value for people they wouldn't want me around and I'd be alone and, as I've mentioned multiple times, I didn't love that idea.

If I removed just those things, I suddenly had about four more hours in my day! What are you doing during the day that you don't *need* to be doing? Take an inventory of your week, on a daily basis, much like people do for their diets. You're going to be surprised, I can almost guarantee it. It's like when parents tell me they got nothing done during the day. I say, "You mean you didn't get everything (or anything) crossed off of your to-do list. Write down everything you *did* do." That list is real long, and it's pretty eye-opening. The fact is, we're either deluding or outright lying to ourselves about how and on what we expend our energy. It's leaving us exhausted and with very little to show for it.

When you've *had* enough, value the Power of the Pause.

I can go from 0-100 with lightning speed. This is a great quality when I wake up and think, "I want to build a garden today." This is not a great quality when I get angry or hurt (when I am hurt, the first emotion I feel is anger). I don't know exactly what happens, but it's not pretty. There's a trigger somewhere deep inside that causes me to want to protect and defend myself at all costs. It's like I'm both the mama bear and her cub simultaneously.

I used to feel great shame in this. I believed it was just how I'm wired. Until I read *Braving the Wilderness* by Brené Brown, that is.

To say my instinctive reaction is "just how I'm wired" is an explanation, not an excuse, and it's critical to know the difference. Much like I use the word "okay" when faced with an interesting challenge or piece of information, I remind myself to pause when I feel myself going to that dark place.

No, it doesn't work 100 percent of the time, but part of the issue had to do with me having greater boundaries in my own life. I really am a happy person, so if someone triggers the part of me that has me lurching for them across the table at Luci's (which, FYI, serves the best gluten-free French Toast in Phoenix), while I have to own my reaction I also have to acknowledge that perhaps that person isn't the healthiest to be around for whatever reason.

If I'm telling myself to pause all day, every day, it's exhausting. And it's a clear indicator that I need to check my crew. If I only have to do it every once in a while and then ask, "Why is this bothering me, and what can I do about it? Is it about me or is it my environment?" it's far more effective.

There is no reason for us to continue to put ourselves in situations where we know we're going to have to pause. Sometimes we have little control over the situation. Perhaps we are in a bad work environment and we need patience while we look for another opportunity. Perhaps we have an ex-spouse who is difficult and from whom we can't fully get away until kids are off to college. Perhaps it's a kid's challenges that are putting us over the edge. But those are also the places where we can grow the very most, precisely because running away from them is not an option.

The greatest challenge I have when it comes to pausing is during face-to-face interactions. Social media interactions? No problem. Thankfully, my fingers don't get all Hear Me Roar and start typing critical comments on posts. You're welcome.

But remember when Kirk told me he thought I was going to end up in a box in an alley, alone and pathetic? (Okay, that's not exactly what he said, but it's what I heard.) Man, did I ever have to pause there. For me, my pause is sometimes simply that—sheer silence. Did you ever notice that "silent" and "listen" contain the same six letters? I don't think this is a coincidence. When we have trouble with one, we usually have trouble with the other and I can most definitely fall into either camp from time to time. I have to remind myself that I don't always have to respond to people on their timelines. I don't have to worry about the fact that *they* are awaiting a response. I have to honor that if they have to get a response right this very second, it's going to come in the form of, "F*ck you, you arrogant piece of shit." They might want a response, but I'm pretty sure they don't want that one! People who know me well know what my pause looks like, and they honor it. People who don't know me well, well, they aren't the ones I'm most worried about honoring by pausing! Oh, and people who know me well don't often put me in an emotional situation that would cause me to need to pause because they know me well enough to know how to phrase things—or when to say nothing at all.

What it comes down to is simple: enough with putting myself in positions wherein I consistently feel I have to defend myself. Enough with spending time with people and places that don't make me smile 99.78 percent of the time. And, if I have to employ the Power of the Pause every time I'm with you, the responsibility lies with me to figure out a solution. And it may just be that our journey, as it's looked thus far, has come to an end.

They say you're the sum of the five people with whom you spend the most time. They also say that each new person you meet is either a reflection of old choices or an indicator of new ones. I love that. I make a decision relatively quickly which category people are in, and I can proudly say that in the last year, I've chosen properly with only a few exceptions because I'm human and people can be unbelievably convincingly great for the first few weeks. It used to be that I chose *poorly* with a few exceptions. So yeah for growth.

TIME TO TAKE ACTION

JOURNAL ACTIVITY

- What are the bright shiny objects in your world?
- What activities do you distract yourself with when you're feeling overwhelmed and/or terrified?
- Are you willing to pay attention to the moments you instinctively seek those activities out and make another choice?

SIX

There's Stuff Everywhere

"Clutter is anything that does not support your better
self."
—*Eleanor Brownn*

wo words I cannot stand (beyond "can't" and "should") are tchotchke and knick-knack. I used to be obsessed with both. I now have neither a need nor a desire for either one. A cluttered house gives rise to a cluttered mind in my world. The state of my kitchen island most days gives you a fairly accurate look at the state of my mind, and it's not pretty.

I remember walking down the streets of Addis Ababa, Ethiopia. It was ten years ago, and I was there to meet my daughter, who was three months old at the time. The moment she was placed in my arms and looked up at me, smiling a smile of pure, unconditional joy (as babies are prone to do) was a game-changer for my spirit. As I walked the city streets with all nine pounds of her in my arms, I noticed kids laughing while playing soccer with a ball made from a plastic grocery bag stuffed with a dozen additional plastic grocery bags. When I'd hand any of them a simple lollipop, they'd act as though they'd won the lottery. And a jar of peanut butter? That was pure gold in their world. They had almost nothing. And they were happier than most kids I see every day in the United States with their brand new clothes, newest model iPhone, and top-of-the-line sports equipment.

We all have too much stuff. Take a look in your closet. If you have anything in there that you haven't worn in at least three years, it's an immediate indicator that you likely need to do a decluttering of your life. During my most recent closet clean-out, I unearthed apparel I've had since the early 2000s. Yes, I know I'm in need of professional help in the form of both a stylist and a personality analyst.

We live in a weird society where we're encouraged to add to our lives in order to create joy. Marie Kondo notably affected our thinking in this area when she penned her bestseller, *The Life-Changing Magic of Tidying Up*. I don't know why anyone was spectacularly surprised by its revelations or its popularity.

For about a decade, my immediate family moved every eighteen months if, for no other reason, because it allowed us the opportunity to look at every single item we didn't know we owned and ask, "Do we need this?" (at least, that's what I told myself during the ten years during which we moved six times). Every time we underwent this exercise, I found myself feeling lighter and lighter. Not just in the number of pounds of crap I had to move from one residence to another but in my soul. Like, who needs all that shit? Amazingly I'm at a point where almost everything in my house has purpose or meaning, and knick-knack is my eighth least-favorite word. It sits right between *fart* and *moist* in the event that anyone was wondering.

Regardless of the fact that Shonda Rhimes wrote the bestselling *The Year of Yes,* in which she agreed to anything and everything for an entire year, a bit of a trend began within which we were encouraged to start saying "No." I think this was just for the requisite yin and yang balance. The minute a group of people start running north, someone has to jump in and yell, "NEW PLAN! IT'S COOL TO RUN SOUTH NOW!" Regardless of the cause, the word No has become all the rage, and I'm all about it.

The first time I intentionally used it was real difficult.

Ironically—but certainly not coincidentally—I happened upon a TEDx talk by Sarri Gilman called Good Boundaries Free You a few days prior. It somehow popped up as my "next video" on YouTube (no idea what I was watching before that), and it looked interesting. Sarri talked all about the importance of being clear on what you say Yes to, what you say No to, and why. She was also clear on the fact that having boundaries decreases anxiety but expressing them creates it. This was a fact I would soon discover.

One of my very best friends in all the world had texted me the night before.

> *Want to go to a Miranda Lambert concert with me next weekend?*

No. No I did not. But I didn't know how to say that, so I left the text unanswered. A few hours later, she texted me again.

> *I guess that's a No. You're probably wondering who the hell Miranda Lambert is!*

Oh, I knew who she is. And it was a firm No. But I didn't know how to tell her that without hurting her feelings. It took fourteen hours for me to respond.

> *I know who she is, but I don't know a single one of her songs!*

"You have a week-plus to learn them," she responded.

My subtle way of excusing myself wasn't working.

> *I think you should take someone to the concert who would truly enjoy it with you! And I want to do something with you so badly! Are you available this Saturday?*

"YOU are going with me!" she said.

Um, this wasn't working.

> *I don't think a Miranda Lambert concert is for me. But can we still do something on Saturday?*

"You are breaking my heart."

Enter the stomach-dropping moment where my worst fears of disappointing my friend were confirmed.

> *I want to hang out with you so badly, I just don't want to go to a Miranda Lambert concert, and I don't want to pretend otherwise! [Insert smiley face and a slew of heart emojis]*

Enter four hours of her not responding and me panicking. I finally texted her back.

> *You aren't truly upset with me, are you?*
>
> No, you doll. It's been a busy day and I have an event tonight. I'll call you tomorrow. [Insert kissy face emoji]

This was a moment, folks.

And before all the Miranda Lambert fans burn this book in effigy, let me state for the record that I'm sure she is completely lovely, and she's clearly got no problem drawing a crowd or finding fans. I'm simply not a country music gal, I don't know a single one of her songs, and the only reason I can bring myself to a concert at this point in my life is a live performance by The Fray, Maroon 5, Imagine Dragons, or Eminem. Even those acts require a pre-concert tranquilizer of some sort combined with a twenty-minute meditation session and a few I'm-fine-everything-is-fine mantras.

I could have told a little white lie, and I knew that. I could have said that David was going hunting or something and so the kids were with me. I could have said I had other plans. I could have claimed an illness that I was sure was going to last for at least the next twelve days.

But I wanted, in that moment, for possibly the first time in my entire life, to respect both the inviter *and* myself enough to honor the truth of why I was saying No.

I was saying No because I DID NOT WANT TO GO!

In her TEDx speech, Sarri was completely on point when she said, "When you listen to your own Yes and No, other people are going to get angry or they may be disappointed. Boundary setting will unleash emotions. And Yes and No are not feelings. So I couldn't let my fear of [someone's] anger or my desire to please [someone] determine my boundaries."

Imagine the ridiculous chain of events that could have happened had I not been honest about my boundaries.

I would have agreed to go to the concert. I would not have looked forward to it. Spending time with my friend? *That* I would have looked forward to. The rest of it? Not so much. It would have been wildly apparent, and she likely would have resented taking me and/or felt I was rude and/or made an incorrect assumption about how I felt about *her* given my demeanor. Then we both would have been upset—me because I was somewhere I didn't want to be, was within an inch of a panic attack, and was resentful of feeling pressured to please my friend, and my friend because she felt like I didn't want to be out and about with her half-heartedly singing about setting fire to a cheating lover's possessions or carrying around the burden of some fragile dude's ego.

In the end, she was fine with me not going. She went with someone who was excited about the opportunity. I spent the evening with cupcakes and a book.

The moment when I found myself not only willing but able to say, "You're important to me *and* I don't want to go to that particular event" and have it be okay will forever remain a defining moment in my life. And considering that this is the same person who taught me to be comfortable saying *I love you*, I suppose it doesn't come as any real surprise that she gave me this gift as well.

When you say No and it truly angers someone, most of the time it's about them, not you. Think about that for a moment. If you don't want to go to a concert or to a specific restaurant or to a club where the music is purposefully loud enough that you can't hear yourself going insane and a friend or partner gets truly angry with you about it, what is really going on? If you ask someone to do something time and time again and they continue to say No and you get angry about it, who are you really angry with? The other person? Or yourself for behaving under the premise that you both view and/or treat the relationship differently than you clearly do?

In this more-more-more world, it's commonplace to find ourselves wondering, "What's next?" But I have to ask, how many social media platforms do we really need? How many different types of lip gloss or razors are really necessary? The other day when I was leaving the gym, I saw a huge ad for a new dating site. This one is called The Lodge. I don't know if it's for outdoor types or people who like sweat lodges or beard oil or what, but it ostensibly has something that makes it different. I can just see the founders sitting in a tent in the middle of nowhere lamenting, "Well, the other 635 dating sites aren't working for everyone, so let's create a new one, shall we?" We're bombarded by podcasts for days, constant livestream notifications, and new, must-have apps beckoning for our more-than-ever divided attention.

We spend much of our time seeking ways to add to our lives. The irony is that, in almost every case, the secret to getting more value, fun, laughter, joy, and worthiness out of our lives is actually getting rid of things! There is only so much space—in our houses, days, and photo storage apps (unless you have the Samsung Galaxy and then, apparently, your storage capacity is endless).

Mindlessly scrolling through social media or bouncing between news stations also creates clutter in my mind (and predominantly negative clutter at that). My best friend Karen now gets her news via Jimmy Fallon's monologue. Can you really blame her? Like, hit me with the highlights, and make them funny please for the love of God.

Somebody help all of us when it comes to email Inboxes. Mine gets out of control more quickly than I can handle. Literally. These days, I take the seven seconds required to immediately unsubscribe to newsletters and offers that don't serve me. Half the time (if not more often) I'm getting the alerts in my Inbox and via text and through my Facebook feed. I choose one or another (or none) but definitely not all three. Trust me, every brand in the universe will give you another opportunity to re-opt-in to their email offers if you're simply devastated at some point by an offer your friend got that you didn't.

Sometimes I think entrepreneurs can be divided into two camps: those who lose their minds if their email Inbox isn't at zero at end of the day or week, and those who don't. (I'll give you one guess regarding into which category Kirk falls). I get the allure of an empty Inbox, I really do. I cannot, however, seem to achieve this goal for more than about forty-eight minutes. I've unsubscribed; I've tried to create folders labeled "To respond," "Important emails," and "Really want to read and might get around to it" to no avail. I have, however, gotten better about keeping the number of emails down. A few months ago, I sent a screenshot of something to Mike, and he responded with the following: "You don't really have 7,580 emails in your Inbox, do you? Because I think I just had a panic attack."

I did, in fact, have that many emails in my Inbox because once you reach a certain level of insanity the amount of time it would take to sort through them all and properly categorize or trash them was not reasonable in my opinion. "Here's what you're going to do," he advised. "Highlight the one at the top. Then Shift + Click on the one at the very bottom. Then click 'Archive.'" As he explained it, this would ensure that none of the emails was trashed in the event that I needed something in there, but it would also clear out my Inbox. So this is exactly what I did. And within thirty-six hours my Inbox was again close to 100 and, given that the name of the game is Zero, I continue to be wildly uncomfortable with the fact that I have an Archived folder with, at present, 5,490 emails in it. But having only sixty-two emails in my Inbox does make me feel surprisingly more capable of breathing, I'll give you that.

In the spirit of sticking with a topic for a moment, let's talk about *why* we get so much email. We sign up for umpteen lists (some voluntarily, some to get a discount code, some we'll never have a clue as to how or when we gave such organizations permission to contact us) and, as a result, get umpteen emails (times ten) on the daily. Now, if you're like I *was*, you simply delete, delete, delete because it's faster than unsubscribing (although only in the short-term). One day, after deleting between thirty and forty such emails in a row, I got religion. I dedicated fifteen minutes to proactively unsubscribing to all emails from brands or companies I hadn't paid attention to since who knows when. If I saw an email from someone I sometimes enjoyed emails from because they were value-filled, I'd delete that specific email but wait to unsubscribe. They had three more shots to keep me as a subscriber. I can now count on two hands the number of email lists I remain on. In many cases, I follow brands thoroughly enough on social media to not need their emailed content. In some cases, it's a constant influx of sales pitches. I have to clear that energetic space to make room for the email wanting to come in from Ellen DeGeneres, right? Because

I'm 99.998 percent sure that's why I haven't yet received one.

Identify your core group of mentors, the ones you find yourself excited to hear from. The whole "I've never read her stuff before, but I might want to someday" is code for "unsubscribe immediately." And for God's sake, if you say, "Who is this person and how did I even get on this list?" it's damn near a universe-given directive to unsubscribe.

Don't worry that one day they might say something that works for you, and if you unsubscribe, you'll miss it. Trust me, if that hasn't yet happened—even once—it probably won't. Not because their message isn't valuable for *someone*; it simply isn't right for *you*. The best thing you can do is find someone who *does* inspire and motivate you in the way that you need to move to the next step of your personal and professional life.

Then there's the art of cleaning out and organizing cupboards full of crap. (That's what they're called in this house. There's the cupboard next to the microwave, the one with the plates, the one under the stove, and the ones full of crap.) Cleaning out and organizing those is literally one of the most satisfying experiences on Earth. I find all sorts of things I thought were lost forever as well as things I don't even know the reason I acquired to begin with. Forget "One day I might latch hook this rug or do this stained-glass art project that cost $1.99 at Michaels and has sat in the cupboard full of crap for four years." If I don't remember putting it in there to begin with, it's going to the trash or the Goodwill. Period.

The number of apps on my phone was equally disturbing. I tried for a while to properly group them. The day I realized I had one grouping titled Health and another titled Workouts with only one app in each folder made it clear that I was trying too hard to organize that which I wasn't even using.

While I commend the UX designer at Apple who said, "We should let the folders of apps scroll for those people who have more than nine apps in a folder" for being so forward-thinking, at the risk of being stingy, if you have more than nine apps in a folder, it's almost as big of a red flag as having clothes from the early 2000s in your closet. I had an entire folder dedicated to Instagram for a time—with two panels. There were eleven apps in total, including three just for reposting. *What if I want that particular reposting app one day?* I thought every time I surfed through the folder. Ohmigod who cares. If I want it, I know where to get it, and there will undoubtedly be seventy-two new, better repost apps available by that point anyway.

While I only had two total apps for Health and Working Out (one of which is the native Health app that cannot be deleted even if I wanted it gone—and I do), I have nine in the folder titled Meditation & Yoga. I clearly had big aspirations in this area. I use only one of them every single day. As in, I only ever use one of the nine. I have one called Peak, and I don't have a clue what is or why I ever downloaded it. But the hell if I'm going to delete it—*I might want to use it someday.*

I just now deleted it.

When you have things in your world—clothes, old emails, apps, latch-hook kits, or an excessive number of but-it-was-on-clearance anythings—that you haven't worn or used in years, it's fair to suggest that you perhaps have trouble letting go of things. And that tendency to hold on tight to things that no longer (or never did) serve you may be spilling over into the way you run your business. You have to let things go in order to make room for the new—personally, professionally, and spiritually.

Get rid of all the noise. There are so many things vying for our attention at every hour of the day, and it's never going to change. In fact, it's only going to get worse. The decision to shut off the noise is just that—a decision. It's a deliberate choice we each have to make, and there's no global right or wrong when it comes to this decision. Your best friend isn't "wrong" for wanting to be on every social media platform, getting a notification every time someone likes her post, or having 27,000 photos in her phone. If it works for her, it works for her. You have to figure out what works for you. How much noise works for *you*? Some people are wildly uncomfortable in complete silence. Some people are uncomfortable if there are more than ten people in a room. What's fascinating is that most of us take on all the noise because we're afraid of missing out. We're afraid of closing ourselves off and not being visible to the "right" opportunities. But, in the end, the less noise you allow into your life, the more your life expands. It's an oxymoron that one tends to only finally believe when he experiences it for himself.

I joined a great thirty-day minimalist challenge once, and one of our first tasks was, "What one thing will you remove from your life today in order to make space for something else?" (It was rightfully argued that if we had everything we wanted in our lives already, we probably wouldn't be in that particular coaching program. Well played.) I didn't identify one thing to remove; I identified three (I like to go above and beyond; have I mentioned that?). I removed myself from an online mastermind group that I truly loved and had gotten a lot of value from but was no longer frequently interacting with. I could benefit by freeing up the financial cost of participating as well as the pressure to "get my money's worth" by making time to jump into the group. I also committed to giving up watching TV at night before bed because I was pretty sure it was messing with my sleep patterns. Finally, I committed to letting go of a personal relationship that was weighing me down and not contributing to my growth.

It's challenging to give things up, especially when they're things to which we've become attached (as in, so attached that we do them without thinking, which is great if they support our growth but awful when they don't, and that is the case most of the time). What's amazing to me is how little we end up missing some of these things and how clear we can become about what they represented to begin with (as well as alternate ways to accomplish those feelings or states of mind).

For the last several decades, I've watched TV before going to bed. I didn't often fall asleep in front of the TV; I'd notice when I was starting to drift off and turn off the TV at that point. But still, I'd wind down by watching TV— usually a sitcom but sometimes something more dramatic.

After hearing for the ninety-seventh time how harmful it is to one's sleep patterns to watch TV or be on your phone within an hour or two of going to sleep, and after one too many mornings wherein a spent the majority of time yawning my way through and wanting to go back to bed (even though I "slept" for eight hours), I decided to try giving up this nightly TV-watching.

But, what will I replace it with? I wondered. I realize that might sound incredibly silly to someone who's never had a TV in her bedroom or who has a different nighttime routine, but any routine is hard to break simply because...well...it's a routine.

I'd recently started a new knitting project, and after knitting two rows, the project simply sat by my bed. I'd chosen that spot on purpose, thinking that if I saw it every day, I'd be reminded to pick it up and work on it. But that's not what happened. I'd see it every day, yes. But I'd also think about how very far I had to go to finish it. It's going to be a blanket and I was two rows in, so you can imagine how long the final project would take to complete.

I wondered, *If I commit to knitting just three rows each night, perhaps I could begin to make some headway.* And so, I did. And when I was finished knitting, I usually wasn't quite ready to go to sleep just yet, so I read. Something entertaining, something educational, something inspiring. I keep a stack of books by my bed that fit each of these categories, and whichever speaks to me is the one I pick up. Yes, I occasionally confuse authors and strategies, but that's where the fun comes in, isn't it?

As entrepreneurs, we have to be able to say No to professional opportunities as well. This can be really hard, especially early on when it's a crap shoot between "Can I pay the bills this month?" and "Do I have to do *that* to pay the bills this month?" Keep in mind that the world at large does not have to be aware of what you're doing "on the side," and letting them know both waters down your brand and confuses long-term and new customers and clients alike.

I'll do whatever I have to do to keep a roof over our heads, keep the kids fed and clothed, and keep the air conditioning on in July—and, to be clear, that statement concludes with "as long as I do it my way." If I decide to work at Starbucks part-time, that will be my decision. (Sidenote: every time my sister calls me and I say I'm working at Starbucks, she says, "So you finally took the plunge, huh?" and I have to clarify that I'm writing a book in Starbucks, not making lattes.)

I started out as a writer just like everyone else, earning my credits and doing things for free to prove myself. But at some point, the $50 per article writing jobs had to go bye bye. They are still in existence, to be sure, and there are plenty of people taking them who don't yet think their writing is worth more than that, which is fine. But the day comes when you simply have to say, "No. I don't do that anymore."

I don't edit manuscripts for $20 an hour anymore (or anywhere near that). I don't write sales copy for $50 an hour anymore. Earlier on, when a month was particularly slow and I needed to pull a rabbit out of a hat to pay the mortgage, I found something I didn't need anymore and sold it, or I made something (and sold it), or I found someone who needed some short-term consulting or project management work done. I just did it all on the down-low while I continued to build my brand and assume the role of a prosperous, impactful, deliriously happy writer and book coach.

In order to make room for something new, most of us have to give up something. Even if we don't yet know what that new something is, the something new we're consciously or unconsciously wanting can't energetically come into our lives if there's nowhere for it to go. It stops by for a second and says, "Hm. I'd like to be in this world, but it's already completely full. There's just no room for me" and moves on to someone else. So the day came when I started saying No to all those cover-me opportunities too. If it wasn't writing- or book-coaching related, I said No. I had to. It was the only way to energetically leave space available for my assumed reality to manifest into the reality I was actually experiencing. It was scary. As. Hell. In fact, it's precisely how I ended up at the aforementioned Day 214.

There are people (although not many) who can attest to the fact that I made this terrifying leap. The reason there weren't many is that I was strategic about who I informed that I was taking this next step. There are a whole lot of incredibly well-meaning people out there who want nothing but the best for me who would have said, "Oh, Liz, just take that other job. It'll let you pay for this or that and then next month you can go back to focusing on your ideal outcome." At some point, you have to keep pushing every single day without having a clue how the reality is going to manifest but with faith, trust, and the utmost belief that it will.

TIME TO TAKE ACTION

JOURNAL ACTIVITY

- Where is the clutter in your physical reality?
- Where is the clutter in your mental/emotional reality?
- What can you give up or let go of in order to make room for something that's in alignment with your North Star?

SEVEN

I Quit

"A river cuts through rock. Not because of its power.
Because of its persistence."
—Jim Watkins

The *how* of building a business absolutely involves strategic and practiced execution, and in my experience, figuring out what stands between you and that kind of strategic and productive execution requires a significant amount of mindset work. We have to either increase our belief in our worth or, in some cases, come down off our high perch. We have to excavate limiting beliefs that are buried so deeply it may very well require an emotional jackhammer to access them. It's easy to grow tired of that work, grow tired of how long it feels like it's taking, and simply quit.

TRUTH BOMB

Resistance to persistence is the root of all endings.
It's one of the worst habits to cultivate. And it comes
from an often deeply hidden comfort with
mediocrity. Because mediocrity is safe.

All my life people have said to me, "Liz, the cool thing
about you is that, if you say, 'I'm going to do such-and-
such,' there's no doubt that you're going to do it." And
they're completely correct. The part they don't realize—
that even I didn't realize until somewhat recently—was
that while I'm great at starting projects, I'm historically
really (really) bad at finishing them.

My mom and I had an unplanned conversation about
this one day. We were discussing the infamous Christmas
lights-untangling story, and I asked her when I went from
being able to sit down and focus for as long as it took to
untangle lights to being so completely all over the place.

She told me that while I spent my younger years
playing Jakbat day-in and day-out—a reality both inspiring
and exhausting for everyone around me—I seemed to lack
the self-discipline to stick long-term with most things.

When I was in elementary school, I played the flute.
According to reports, I was pretty good. One day, I decided
I wanted a piccolo. My mom emptied her fun-money
account to buy me a piccolo. I played it twice.

I took up horseback riding around the same time
because my best friend was extremely good at it. I was just
okay. I had a panic attack every time I had to reach under

the horse's belly to grab the girth, and I had night terrors over getting kicked in the face as I cleared matted grass and mud from the horse's shoes, but I suppose I had promise given that none of the instructors said, "Sorry, you are hopeless. Get out." My poor mother again emptied her fun-money account to ensure that I had proper riding pants and boots, and it wasn't long before I was paired up with DJ, who stood eighteen hands tall. For those of you not familiar with equestrian terminology, DJ was one big-ass horse.

DJ And I bonded. Or at least I thought we did. One day, I went for my lesson; grabbed the saddle, girth, and bridle from the tack room; got DJ all ready to go; and proceeded to begin trotting around the indoor ring as my mom and sister watched from the sidelines. I don't know what the hell was wrong with DJ that day, clearly it wasn't a good day for him, but he was making some strange noises, and at one point he began galloping. I had not instructed him to do that. I also hadn't cinched his girth tightly enough. Before he'd gone fifteen feet, I'd slid left and was riding on his side—not his back—with the wall quickly approaching. Instinct took over and I bailed, off of DJ and out of my horseback riding pastime. Seriously, I'm pretty sure I stood up, and as my instructor said, "Okay, Liz, get back in the saddle" I was already, "Mom, I'll meet you in the car. Peace out, DJ."

I became interested in tennis in high school (which may have had something to do with the fact that the number one player for a rival high school's team was extremely cute). I'm not a naturally gifted athlete, and I was far from the best player on the team. My closest friend, however, *was* the best player on the team. Did I ask her to play with me once a week for practice? Did I spend time on the weekends perfecting my serve? Nope. I just moved on to the cross-country running team (which didn't end successfully either. Stay tuned.). A short while ago, I watched a documentary about Serena Williams wherein I learned that she hates working out. What I took from this revelation was that I could have become the number one tennis player in the world if I'd stuck with it. My sense that loving exercise was a prerequisite to being a successful tennis player was completely off base. How disappointing.

When I was a junior in college, I bought myself a guitar. I invited over a friend who'd been playing all his life and asked him to give me my first lesson. We sat on the front steps of my apartment building, he taught me where to place my fingers to play a C chord, and dammit all to hell those strings were going to slice through my fingers before I learned to play Hot Cross Buns. I was sure of it. He told me he wouldn't teach me another chord until I'd played that one for a week. That meant that I wouldn't be able to play like Eric Clapton by the weekend, so I sold the guitar.

When I started businesses earlier in life, I had one clear and immediate goal: get rich. Not even kidding. Oh, also, get rich in 2.4 minutes or less because otherwise I got bored. I'm the most impatient person you've ever met, I promise. I'm constantly working on it and recognize that "get rich" is not even remotely close to a clearly attainable goal with a solid *why* behind it.

And yet, because it didn't happen in 2.4 minutes, I quit.

I—as well as most entrepreneurs—tend to occupy close quarters with multiple What ifs: What if this business never truly launches? What if I spend years of my life focusing on this and it goes nowhere? What if I have to tell people that I failed? What if I lose all credibility? What if I end up sleeping in an alley behind Whole Foods, living as one of those freegan folks? What if freeganism is no longer even a lifestyle? What if everyone can look at me, smirk, and say, "I told you she'd never get anywhere with that." And let's not neglect, *What if it actually does go somewhere and then people are depending on me in two-week increments for their livelihood?*

Surprisingly perhaps, the successful version of "what if" is the way in which it manifested earlier in my life. What if I learn to play piccolo really well, and I'm asked to join the symphony, and I don't want to do that? What if I learn to play tennis really well, and I have to go on tour with Andre Agassi, and I don't know what to say to him? What if I get this horseback riding thing down, and I have to jump really high gates...competitively...while people are watching? No thank you. What if I master this guitar, and I'm asked to go on tour with an up-and-coming band, and I'm not skinny enough to wear leather pants? What if this business launches and I get really rich, and I don't know who my real friends are versus who's just hanging out with me because I'm really rich?

My perceived glass ceiling was the *beginning* of actual success. It was the growth phase. I was terrified of growth because I had no idea what it looked like or how to navigate it. So I subconsciously self-sabotaged in order to make damn sure that I never reached that point.

Now, out of fairness to and love for myself, I'd like to point out that there are a few surprising areas where I did, in fact, stick with something until it was completed. Twenty years ago, I gifted my mom with a large counted cross-stitch piece of artwork. I know exactly what prompted me to choose such a large pattern, and that is the fact that I do nothing on a small scale. What prompted me to actually *complete* the thing, however, I can't say. Interestingly, my mom reports that even she, who has done counted cross-stitch since forever, might not have taken on such a large, elaborate pattern, and the thing is damn near perfect. I'd like to point out that while I didn't remember working on the piece until she recently reminded me of it, I do now remember in vivid detail how intricate it was. There were moments I absolutely could not believe what I'd gotten myself into, but I simply refused to quit until it was not only finished but a sight to behold, even if that meant ripping out entire sections and starting again because I'd done a stitch backward at some point.

Another hobby I took up about eighteen years ago is knitting. I remember this day with remarkable clarity as well.

Sidenote: Memory is an interesting concept. I have no idea what I had for lunch yesterday, but I remember the story I'm about to tell you as though it happened five minutes ago.

My sister, Katie, was in town visiting, and out of nowhere we decided to become knitters. Our mom has knit since forever (right along with her counted cross-stitch adventures; she had an in-process knitting project as well as a counted cross-stitch project at her feet while she watched TV at almost all times). We hopped into the car; drove to Michaels craft store; and purchased a how-to-knit instruction book, yarn, and some needles.

We then sat on my family room floor and followed the instructions as best we could. It was slow-going. It wasn't nearly as easy as our mom made it look, but I was committed. Katie, not so much. After about ninety minutes wherein the only words coming from her mouth were, "What the hell" and "Ouch!" she said, "Screw it. I quit. Look, I made an eyebrow warmer." At which point she held a row of seven or eight (poorly) knit stitches over her eyebrow before tossing the needles to the ground in disgust.

I wasn't particularly pleased at how long it was taking to get a decent-looking row, but I remember my mom advising, "Just knit for fifteen minutes each day. In two weeks, you'll be off to the races." *Two entire weeks?* Somehow, for some reason, I took up this challenge, and lo and behold, after two weeks I was knitting a pretty gorgeous something-or-other. My sister blames her defeat on the fact that she's left-handed, and the instructions were not intended for a lefty, but I'd like to point out that my ten-year-old daughter taught herself to knit last month. She's a lefty. And she knits right-handed. When I told her she could do it with a left-handed method, her response was, "Well this is what the YouTube instructions said to do, and it's working so..."

The minute I recognized that I had the knit and purl stitches down pat, I purchased a pattern for a floor-length sweater coat because why the hell would I start with something simple like a scarf? That sweater coat is nowhere near finished and it's been eighteen years. I doubt the style is even still relevant. Come to think of it, it's probably gone out of style and come back in by this point. But I'm happy to report that I've knit sweaters for friends' babies—with cowl necks, folks—and prayer shawls and baby hats and I'm working on a set of matching sweaters for my friend's Pugs (without cowl necks; I'm never doing that again).

The only reason I can come up with as to why I stuck with knitting and cross-stitch (at least long enough to complete the project; I've never cross-stitched another thing and never will) is that there was no true fear of failure with these projects. I certainly wasn't relying on them for income, and the recipients didn't know I was making what I was making until they were presented with it, so the only person who would know if I quit was me. I was competing only with myself and, apparently, I'm pretty good at that as long as I don't publicize it!

On another side note, I took up knitting when the concepts of YouTube, FaceTime, and Skype didn't yet exist, so I'd call my mom (the only other person I knew who knit) when I got into a "situation" (the cowl neck on the baby sweater involved many such moments). I didn't even say hello. I just launched with, "So I'm taking the needle from southwest to northeast and then wrapping the yarn counterclockwise twice and then I'm pulling the right needle down until only one of the wraps can be looped back over and then..."

My mom quickly lost almost every ounce of joy she initially felt over the fact that I was sticking with something. It got to the point that she'd request that I give her twenty minutes' notice before such calls so she could brew coffee and take three ibuprofen.

Also, Katie recently posted the following on Facebook: "Who knows how to knit or crochet and wants to teach me? Extra points if you're a lefty!" I was like, "Are you freaking kidding me? Imagine how good you could be today if you hadn't quit after completing that half-hearted eyebrow warmer?" (Yes, I hear myself.) So now she and I have an agreement: in an effort to compel her to keep going after she's knit something the size of her eyebrow, we've committed to knitting each other's Christmas presents. She promptly sent me a picture of a crocheted dress featured on Pinterest that she plans to make me in the next four months. I will not be outdone, so I'm knitting her a car.

You've likely seen the meme illustrating the reality of life for entrepreneurs or otherwise creative people. It looks like a Swiss mountain range and features the commentary: "This is amazing. I'm not really sure about this. This is absolute crap. I have an idea. I feel really good about this. What was I thinking? Maybe if I just... I'm on fire now. I feel it all coming together. I don't feel good about this. Somebody kill me. Oh! I've got it!"

This is all of us on a weekly (if not hourly) basis, whether we are willing to publicly admit it or not. So relax because you're totally normal. I'm relatively sure that even Ellen DeGeneres still has these moments. Maybe not.

I didn't miss the pinnacle of my version of success with the Hold It Baby or the various consulting services or the bird watcher's website (don't ask) or the idea for sunscreen that actually smells good (yes, it is a good idea) because any of those ideas was inherently bad or I wasn't the right person to be in that space or I didn't have the right credentials or know the right people. In fact, I'm pretty good at networking, and I'm pretty sure that skill is responsible for my getting hired once without anyone even looking at my resume. I also suppose one could argue that each of my businesses *was* successful in that I at least launched it. But in terms of being enough for *me*, none of them reached their full potential for one main and inarguable reason: I gave up. And I gave up because I was terrified of both success and failure. That moment of giving up was, therefore, the one and only guarantee that existed for many years, completely unbeknownst to me.

No one can, with believability, suggest that fewer than three years is a reasonable amount of time to commit to building a sustainable, scalable business. I remember once when Gary Vee was asked by someone whether he should quit his business-building plan because it simply wasn't going anywhere.

Gary asked, "How long have you been at this?"

"Four months."

Gary's response was simple and direct: "Fuck off."

The new cool thing is to be a rule-breaker, a path-forger, a race leader, a unicorn. Armed with little more than fierce determination and a budget for vats of coffee, newly self-declared entrepreneurs everywhere mount their rented-by-the-hour city bicycle and ride off to the nearest co-working space, vowing to make it work via "my way or the highway."

They've visualized their dream. But they are not even remotely prepared to do what's necessary to get from where they are to where they desire to go. And so we again see them, a mere three months later, forlorn and crying into their grande macchiato on the side of said highway while lamenting their complete lack of understanding as to why the 500,000 fans they purchased for $10.99 or the seven-hour-long unfocused days they invested over the past twelve weeks haven't paid off in spades. And, to be clear, I was absolutely a part of this club for quite some time. I'm not judgmentally describing a foolish group of people; *I was a card-carrying member of this group* (though I've never rented a city bicycle).

For real, if a person could build a successful, sustainable, scalable business in an average of four months, don't you think we'd all be massively wealthy business owners? Most people simply don't have (or choose to cultivate) the perseverance (read: self-discipline) required. Their work ethic doesn't match their ambition and/or their mindset is jacked up. They get caught up thinking that by having a "bridge" job to pay bills while they're building their dream, they are somehow not a "real" entrepreneur. They're afraid that if they don't have venture capitalists on speed dial or find themselves sitting in the first class cabin every other weekend they'll be seen as a fraud or are flat-out doing something wrong.

Go back in time and review the journey of any entrepreneur who has found the level of success to which you aspire, and you will see years and years of work and sweat and pivots and re-evaluations and fuck-this-shit moments. It's never overnight. And when it is, by sheer coincidence (and not the cosmic kind), it never lasts because the entrepreneur isn't prepared mentally or emotionally to keep it going at full throttle.

Look at Marie Forleo. The woman is killing it! But look back twelve or so years ago when she was getting started. She went to her day job and then came home and made videos from her computer in her tiny NYC apartment. Gary Vee? He started making videos for his wine library, and they were watched by two, three, maybe four people. He stayed consistent, tweaked when necessary, but JUST KEPT GOING. He always knew his *what* and his *why*. The business changed into an agency from a wine company (though he still works with the family's wine company), but he followed his own *why* no matter what he was doing. Whether he was making videos about wine or hilarious, energy-filled motivational videos in taxi cabs, he executed at 100 percent.

Perseverance, determination, self-discipline, work ethic—call it whatever you want. At its core, it's the "thing" that compels you to do the "things" you don't want to do at precisely the moment when you don't want to do them. It's the only reason I enter the gym. Ever. It's the result of having an extraordinarily strong *why* and being completely unavailable for any other outcome—even when you and your entire family and circle of friends worry that you may have legit lost your mind.

My fascination with the backstories of entrepreneurs is also the basis for the way I work with them to get their books written. I love hearing about the hardships they've navigated—not because I'm glad anyone had them but because if he or she didn't have them it's going to be really hard to identify with them as a human being. If someone has gone through trials and tribulations on the way to success and still achieved her dreams, I know that I can too. I love the unique way we are each shaped by what we experience, and how we choose to use those experiences as steps to elevate to the next level.

The five stages of business (in case you missed the lesson the first time) are Idea, Start up, Growth, Expansion, and Maturity. The reason I didn't previously get to the Expansion (and, therefore, Maturity) stage is that I didn't have the required self-discipline to get into the Growth phase. Everyone has their own personal trigger for getting "stuck" in a stage. For me, it was fear of growth. Or no growth. I'm not a tall person, so maybe it has roots there. Regardless, the only thing that could be guaranteed by my lack of focus and discipline is that my fears would always win, and I'd never truly know what authentic "growth" or "non growth" even looked like.

TIME TO TAKE ACTION

JOURNAL ACTIVITY

- What was the last thing, big or small, that you quit before you reached your desired outcome?
- What fear caused you to quit (because if you *knew* without a doubt that you'd reach success, you wouldn't have quit, right)?
- How can you take an intentional step each day to combat this fear?

EIGHT

I'll Do It Later

"Indecision and delays are the parents of failure."
—*George Canning*

Distractions are persuasive, and coincidentally, so is familiarity. Our ego is kind of an a-hole. It wants to keep us safe, so it talks us out of doing all kinds of things that are outside of our comfort zone but that we also *need* to do in order to grow. Sometimes, people are unaware of their ego because they've allowed it to hide behind miles and miles of bravado. This is what is happening much of the time when you encounter someone who's incredibly arrogant or an outright liar when it comes to his or her accomplishments and credentials.

Have you heard of paralysis by analysis? Of course you have. It's about as rampant a mindset as "I can't" or "I should," and it's one of the leading symptoms of a lack of self-discipline—the kind of self-discipline that will get you from where you are to where you envision yourself ending up. It's important to have a general idea of where to start, I'll give you that. Throwing darts against random dart boards hoping that they stick and lamenting, "Well, at least I'm taking action" is a waste of time, plain and simple. However, many times we spend so much time analyzing how to do something the exact perfect way that we do flat-out nothing. It doesn't have to be perfect to be done. And it sure doesn't have to be perfect to get started!

There is a fine line between having a plan of attack and waiting for that plan to be so honed that it becomes nothing more than an excuse for why you never take action. I've worked with clients who say, "As soon as I decide which book to write, I'll start." Just pick one! Draw it out of a hat if you have to! In almost all cases, paralysis by analysis is the result of fear (shocking, right?). After all, if you don't start, you can't ever fail. You have to accept that never starting is its own form of failure.

When I was twenty-seven, I decided unequivocally what I wanted to be when I grew up. If you've read *You Cannot Be Serious*, you've heard this story before, so you can fast forward a few paragraphs if you'd like.

I determined that my ideal career was that of a speech language pathologist. I wanted to become fluent in sign language and work with children who were born deaf, had received cochlear implants, and were learning to hear and speak instead of using sign language.

I nearly lost my mind with excitement when I thought about the opportunity to spend all day every day working with children with hearing loss. And one day, it was decided: I'd go back to school to take the pre-requisites required to apply to graduate school so that I could get my master's degree and start practicing. Man, was I excited.

And then I got out of the dream and into the particulars.

It would take a year to complete the pre-requisites (while raising three kids under the age of three). Then three years of grad school. Probably an internship. I was going to be thirty-one or thirty-two before I could even start practicing. It felt like so far in the future. Thirty-one or thirty-two sounded so *old*.

There were several reasons I didn't pursue the career beyond that, but the thematic *I can't have it right now* factor was likely the biggest deterrent. And yet, those years went by anyway. Had I pushed through, I'd probably have my PhD by now and would have been in practice for fourteen or so years. (Don't do the math, please. Thanks.).

Perhaps ironically, nearly everyone I talk with (whether friends or clients) has dozens of areas they'd like to explore, businesses they'd like to start, or hobbies they'd like to undertake. But when it comes time to get started, we also have a million reasons to simply lie down and take a nap.

The universe works in magnificent ways, but one thing it does not do is say, "Oh, Liz, that's a cool idea. Please open your front door; it's sitting there waiting for you. See how easy that was?"

More often than not, the universe will allow you to take three steps toward your dreams only to violently yank you one step back like a sick game of Chutes and Ladders just to test how badly you really want it. The reason most people don't reach their dreamed-about destination is that they give up on the final leg. The universe has a funny way of providing you with the greatest test right before you reach the finish line just to see if you're *truly* ready and if you *truly* want what you claim to want. The number of people who have quit (myself included) when they were literally one tweak from their definition of success is surely staggering.

TRUTH BOMB

If you simply dream while sitting on your ass, all you'll ever have to show for it is the world that lives in your imagination.

Once we make the decision about what we're going to tackle, we have to make a secondary decision to stop making excuses and drop the wait already. We have to remove from our vocabulary, "I'll figure this out when...", "I'll explore it when..." and "I'll get to it after..."

You're more than welcome to continue making those excuses, but the thing is, life has a way of getting in there and making you take charge even if you aren't completely ready. The real challenge that then occurs is, you're trying to figure *yourself* out while figuring out the situation in which you've found yourself.

There's a reason we procrastinate and are slow to master self-discipline. It's not because we aren't good enough or smart enough or likable enough. It's because we're...wait for it...afraid. Now, I can't tell you for sure exactly what you're afraid of, but I can tell you with absolute certainly that you are afraid of *something*. Whether it's success or failure or others' perceptions or being responsible or letting someone down or letting yourself down, you're putting off getting started because you are subconsciously convincing yourself that, by waiting, you are delaying your greatest fear: inevitable disappointment.

I remember about ten years ago when I thought for sure I was ready to be a millionaire with tons of clients and notoriety (we all think we're ready for this long before we actually are). Fast forward six or seven years, and boy was I glad that the level of success I previously hoped for didn't happen back then. Because I was in *no way* ready. I didn't know who I was. I didn't know what was really important to me. I didn't know what I was buying or wearing or doing based on who I was versus who I thought everyone else wanted and expected me to be. It would have added a complicated layer to an already complicated existence. I now understand how important it is to be in one's rightest mind, the most prepared he or she can possibly be, surrounded by all the "right" people, when that level of success hits.

Stop putting off the art of figuring it all out. Stop thinking that it will figure itself out all on its own. I swear, I used to think that if I ignored the dishwasher long enough, it would empty itself. Stop thinking of all the reasons you can't do it. Stop thinking of all the reasons it won't work. Stop thinking of all the "bad" things that could happen. Because what if none of those bad things happens? What if you step right into the life you are meant to live? What if you step into the fullest and most amazingly whole version of yourself? Ponder *that* What If for a moment.

Most people are waiting on one of three things (or two, or all three) to take the next step in starting a venture or moving it forward: time, money, and knowledge. Waiting for the right time is literally pointless. Just when you think you've reached it, a new to-do will present itself; it's just how the universe works. We're all "super busy," but busy with what? I'll tell you what: we're all super busy claiming to be super busy! Seriously, there is no "perfect time" for anything. Not for getting married or having a baby or adopting a dog or painting your kitchen cabinets. There may be a clear "wrong" time for certain things, but if you're waiting for all the stars to align or thinking, "I'll do this when..." you would do well to examine your underlying fear because what you're really waiting for is that fear to abate, which simply won't happen until you look it in the eyes. If you claim not to have enough time, do the exercise nutritionists do with their clients' diets: write down everything you do each day for an entire week. I guarantee you'll find some spots you can fill with something that's more productive and in line with your professional goals as well as your personal and spiritual growth.

If money is what you're waiting on, let me tell you, money is like a river. It flows. No, I'm not encouraging you to go out and spend $5,000 on something when your credit card bills are already through the roof and you're living on a diet of Rice Krispies. What I'm saying is that there are areas where you could likely cut back or bring in "just enough" to begin working toward your dream. People seem to believe it's all or nothing; invest in the $5,000 coaching program or invest in no coaching program at all. What happened to a great $97 coaching program? (They are out there, believe me.) What happened to a $47 online workshop that will help you get clarity in a particular area? If you're waiting for money, what can you sell on eBay? Can you create a crowdfunding campaign? What can you do on the side to start bridging the gap? A few dollars here and there quickly add up.

When my writing clients say, "I failed today because I didn't write 2,500 words," I ask, "Well, how many words *did* you write?" They inevitably say, "Zero." There's a lot of space between zero and 2,500! You have to create the self-discipline to be able to respond with a number other than zero because, trust me, you probably won't feel like writing most days (until you're in the midst of it, at which point the whole activity gets far more exciting). Just because you can't go all in doesn't mean you can't dip a toe in and make some progress toward your goal. When we wait for everything to align perfectly, we set ourselves up to wait forever, and I honestly think that's some people's strategy: simply be able to say, "The timing was never right."

Bullshit.

The timing is both never right and always right. You are giving away all of the power when you claim that the stars didn't properly align in your lifetime. You simply have to start looking at them from a different angle.

As for "I don't have enough knowledge," get ready because I'm about to get on a big old soapbox. I hear all the time, "I don't have the right credentials to do that." Yes, there are some career areas in which you need bonafide credentials. No one is cutting me open with a scalpel without a degree from a medical school, preferably in this country. You aren't going to be a licensed ophthalmologist without formal study; you don't learn that stuff on YouTube.

But there is a big gray area as well. Some of the world's most successful (by financial and status-based measure, anyway) CEOs didn't graduate from college. Most of the experts I follow have degrees that would make you laugh because they are wildly far from their actual area of expertise. The bottom line: they've studied. Not formally at an Ivy League institution graduating Summa Cum Laude per se, but they've read. And attended seminars. And had or developed the self-discipline to do practical work daily. And networked. And watched videos. And taken online trainings. And they don't only know their area in the sense that they are "book smart," they have also applied all of their learnings so they really, truly understand that of which they speak.

A $250,000 college education can't buy that. And no, I'm not suggestion that you avoid a college education. That's another discussion entirely. What I'm suggesting is that, if your defense is, "I'm not credentialed enough" and what you aren't credentialed enough to do doesn't involve saying, "Suction please" or studying people's brain waves while they're in space, you're simply afraid that someone else is going to tell you that you aren't knowledgeable enough. I have a degree in Japanese. I have that credential. However, if someone hired me today based on that fact alone, they'd be sorely disappointed because the only Japanese phrases I remember at this point are "What time is it?", "Which direction do I go?" and "You're a fucking idiot."

Most of the time, we put off our dreams because they feel overwhelming. We're afraid of "failing," we're afraid of not finishing (in other words, failing), we're afraid of disappointing someone (in other words, failing).

But what if we didn't "fail?" What if we finished and pleased ourselves instead of all of the "other people" whose opinions we think we're worried about?

What is everyone waiting for? More money? More time? Better weather? Their office to be finished? These are all reasons I both hear and have given time and time again. And they're superficial because they don't address the real issue that's causing you to wait. You've surely heard the phrase, "What would you attempt if you knew you would not fail?" Well, what if you had a crystal ball and you knew that you would not fail? What if you knew that doors would open and you'd grow and heal and be better no matter the minute details of the outcome? Were that the case, wouldn't you have started already? Wouldn't you work through the "...but I don't want to do this today" moments?

Of course you would.

It's not that any "thing" is too overwhelming. It's that we need a better approach. Or we need to address a deep-seated fear. Or both. But getting to the root of the problem—not just the symptom of the problem—is the key that unlocks a world of possibilities.

SHORTCUT TO ENOUGH

Ask yourself what you're waiting for. Whatever the answer is, ask, "What if that were accomplished today?"

You'll quickly find your own arguments losing weight, thereby allowing your timeline to lose wait as well.

TIME TO TAKE ACTION

JOURNAL ACTIVITY

- What have you been procrastinating?
- What's something you were once interested in doing or committing to that you bailed on because it felt like it would take so long?
- If you'd started then, how far ahead would you be now?
- Are you willing to commit to choosing ONE of the things you've been procrastinating on and focus on tackling a little bit each day for the next 100 days?

NINE

I'm Overwhelmed and Terrified

"The person determined to achieve maximum success learns the principle that progress is made one step at a time."
—*David J. Schwartz*

I t can be wildly overwhelming to stand at the starting line. At first, it's exhilarating. You're there. If you're me, you're dressed accordingly whether it's the starting line of a marathon or the top of a snow-covered mountain. Even though I've never snowboarded, the day I do, believe you me, I'll have on all the right gear. I'll be crashing and burning every three seconds, but I will be wearing cool gear while doing it. When I participated in CrossFit a few years ago I complained so loudly that they almost kicked me out a few times—but I always showed up in my Lululemon attire. Dress the part, people.

Anyway, you're standing at the starting line (which, for this analogy, let's presume is the top of the snow-covered mountain) in your fashionable snowboarding pants and cool hat, and then you look down. It's a long way down. There are lots of bumps and people you could get tangled up with and trees you could snowboard smack into. There are so many things that could go wrong between that gorgeous view at the top and being safely and securely at the bottom, ready to go again. This feeling makes most of us sit down, detach from the snowboard, and make snow angels instead.

As I've stated, I love DIY projects, but fortunately or not, I don't take on small projects. A DIY project in my world does not involve hanging pictures on the wall or painting a laundry room. It's reconstructing entire rooms, building built-in furniture, laying tile, and wiring electric. (yes, I consult with an electrician, like, 94 percent of the time). I just don't do small. And, as I've explained, I rarely have a plan when I set out. I find this is the case in most areas of my life. I'm kind of a "wing it" girl.

In some ways, this is super beneficial. When things don't go according to plan, it's okay because there wasn't actually a plan to begin with. In some ways, it creates chaos. Challenges that could have been foreseen and solved early via a plan require time-consuming fixes and re-work. I'd love to say, "Next time I do this I'll know how to do it properly," but the truth is, there will not be a next time for the vast majority of the DIY projects I undertake!

I recently installed either distressed wood or shiplap on three separate walls of my house—one in my bedroom, one in my office, and one in the family room. All three of these walls were done differently (because, come on, doing them the same way would be too easy). For my bedroom wall, I used 1 x 4s, all of which I individually sanded and stained a variety of colors. My office wall is pre-fab shiplap, and my family room wall is a shiplap-type look made from pre-cut plywood (bless the nineteen-year-old at Lowe's named James who agreed to cut all of it for me one Friday night).

When I got started with each wall, I had the same thought: "This won't be too bad." In each case, I was intensely mistaken.

The bedroom wall was challenging, mostly because it is on the second floor and the miter saw is in the garage, so I had to go up and down a flight of stairs each time I had to make a cut. All the sanding and staining was also time-consuming. And then there was the moment I realized that I had to figure out how to re-wire the outlets so they didn't sink behind the wood—that added a few days to the project.

The office wall was demanding because genuine shiplap isn't always easy to work with, and I'm a perfectionist. The family room wall was, in many ways, the easiest. (Having done two walls already, I had a bit of knowledge on a few tips that would make it easier and knew of a few roadblocks to avoid.) That said, when I first got started, I looked at the wall and thought, "That's a big wall. But this should go fairly quickly." There are two windows on the wall that had to be framed out and then worked around. The first board I had to install required that I cut out space for the window header I'd just built. Do you think I made the cut properly?

By this point, I hope you didn't say yes or you really haven't been paying attention.

Not only did I mess it up once; I messed it up twice. Suddenly, my "this will go fairly quickly" project felt heavy. I couldn't even get the first board up properly. But hey, only 55 to go!

I got through the first row, which required three boards (two of which had to be cut to accommodate windows), and after starting on the second row, I thought, "Okay, I'm in a groove now. Not a problem."

Four hours later, exhausted, bleeding on both a finger and a toe, and covered in sawdust, I was only halfway finished. It was hard in that moment to see the cup as half full because the wall was half empty!

I said, "One more board, and then I'll take a break."

I put up one more board and walked to the mailbox. When I got back from the mailbox, I looked at the wall and said, "One more board and then I'll switch the laundry." I put up one more board and switched the laundry. And on it went with the philosophy of "One more board..." until I realized that, one board at a time, I'd managed to get the wall 75 percent finished.

We are spectacularly talented at looking at the end goal and getting excited. We are equally good at having all the energy, positivity, and enthusiasm required at the starting line. Where we get tangled up is somewhere in the middle. That's when we become highly overwhelmed and terrified. But time's going to go by anyway, so we might as well make the most of it!

One board at a time. One word at a time. One chapter at a time. It's how this book is getting written for heaven's sake! One pound at a time, one inch at a time, one second at a time. It's why I tell my writing clients, no matter how many words you wrote yesterday, write *one* more today. That's it! Increase by one every single day. It's the same concept as making one extra car payment or mortgage payment per year. It feels like a small step, but combined, it moves you closer to your goal with intention, clarity, and subtle shifts over a period of time. You don't even notice the new habits you're creating. One day, you write 500 words. Ninety days later, you're writing 591 words. The addition of that one extra word (or ten, or twenty) each day compounds and gets you to your goal sooner while continuing to build a beneficial habit.

It's much like putting together a puzzle (literally and figuratively). When you start working on a 1,000-piece puzzle, it feels completely overwhelming. This is why I start with the edges. When I get to a spot that's all white, for example, and I want to kill myself, I try the available pieces one at a time. When I find the one that fits, I move to the next and begin the process again.

How long it will take to complete the puzzle is based on a few things, not the least of which is how many pieces you work to place in a day and whether or not, after putting piece number forty-six in place, you see another puzzle in the closet and get it out. If you are consistent about placing ten puzzle pieces per day, you will finish in a specific number of days. If you only put a piece in when you feel like it, you'll likely never finish. I know this because we had a puzzle on our kitchen table for about four months this year until, one day, I said, "Nope. It has to get finished. I need my table back." Five hours and zero help later, she was done.

There's an old story about a frog being put into warm water and the water being slowly heated until the frog is actually boiling. The frog never realizes he is boiling because the water temperature is increased so gradually. I see this happen in people's lives as well—their "normal" gradually becomes so absurd that they still see it as normal while everyone around them wonders how they are still upright. The same dynamic can work to our benefit as well, however. Add an extra word, an extra pushup, an extra burpee (you won't see me doing that one), an extra twenty steps on the mountain, an extra page read, an extra row knitted every single day—take this approach and watch your work not only grow quickly but your incorporation of that new approach take hold to the point that it becomes your new lifestyle.

We have a book-writing bootcamp within the Publish A Profitable Book framework, and Week One always starts strong. Participants are excited and have a ton of positive energy for the work they are about to embark upon.

Week One often usually finishes strong as well. Toward the end of Week Two, something starts to happen. People start to slip. They start to feel the weight of the task they've taken on. Maybe they're used to writing 3,500 words per day, but they aren't used to writing memoir. Perhaps they got those 2,500 words out on Days One through Three, but now the thoughts are coming more slowly and they're watching as the word count they are supposed to be at goes higher and higher while they fall further and further from the goal. They watch those around them write 1,000 words a day or 2,000 words a day while they're only mustering fifteen. They decide that "it's just not a good time for this," and want to quit. I say "want to" on purpose because I don't let my boot campers quit. I haven't had one successfully quit yet. We fix a mindset or restructure a day's schedule, but quitting is not an option unless someone says, "I sincerely do not want to write a book anymore" and explains why. That has not yet happened. May this statement not jinx that.

Most often, the tweak is not that they have to carve out more time in their day or eliminate *Game of Thrones* or *Stranger Things* from their schedule. It's that their *enough* has to be modified. The have fallen prey to believing that they haven't done enough by writing a certain number of words, when the truth is that they have done enough simply because they've continued on. I tell people, "Write fifty words today. Write ten. I don't care. Just have more written at the end of today than you did when the day started." That is enough. One step (or, in this case, word) at a time, you'll get to your goal. Just keep going.

What they are resisting is that they need to hone a particular habit. What we are making sure of is that, even though they started the marathon with tons of energy, and even though they got to mile twenty in a lot of pain, they kept going. They walked if they had to. Crawled if they had to. But they kept going. They may not have finished with the best time, but they finished. Everyone may have gone home already, but it doesn't change the fact that they can now say, "I finished a marathon."

Know for each year what your *enough* is and break it down into quarters so that you have measurable action steps and goals against which you can measure, pivot, and reassess as necessary to reach that goal. This helps to keep overwhelm at bay. I'm a huge fan of the word pivot, and I give all the credit to Ross Geller from *Friends*. Beyond saying it, I'm a huge fan of *doing* it and recognizing that it doesn't represent quitting in the least; it represents an acceptance of reality combined with one's own limits and lifestyle.

Pivoting and quitting are two very different concepts. Pivoting occurs when you realize something isn't working as expected, ascertain why, and put a new system in place. Pivoting is saying, "This ad strategy isn't working and I need to figure out why." Quitting is saying, "This product sucks and I'm done with it entirely. Someone find me a new URL to reserve by noon." Quitting is throwing the baby out with the bathwater (someone please tell me who coined that term because it's just weird).

Properly pivoting is both an art and a science. It requires that you are decidedly clear on your methods and that both your strategy and process are clearly defined. For example, an ad platform was developed somewhat recently called AdEspresso. It's fantastic. It takes all of your ad headlines, images, and copy and creates as many variables of them as you'd like in order to test what works best for a particular audience. You can then combine the most popular headline, copy, and image and scale your campaign as you identify the most receptive audience. Many people take this to the extreme, however. They put everything and the kitchen sink into an ad possibility and serve it up to a variety of audiences. They cast the widest net possible. And then when they go to analyze the data, they've blown through their $5,000 ad budget, have no idea why it didn't work, and can't put their finger on what one thing makes the most sense to change. Because if you change more than one thing at a time, you don't know which change is responsible for the new data. It requires patience, precision, and persistence, all of which are necessary in equal amounts!

I remember hearing that Facebook ads would only work if I invested $3,000 per month in them. I simply could not do that at the time, so I said, "No. I'll find another way." True, $5 per day does take a long while to rack up enough data to allow for thoughtful analysis, but I somehow created a miracle and employed patience. Six months later, I could identify common patterns in one single audience and scale from there. Was it ideal? Of course not. But just because you aren't able to do something the way someone says you have to doesn't mean you can't do it at all. Properly pivoting also requires that you understand why you're doing so and what your new goal/approach is.

TIME TO TAKE ACTION

JOURNAL ACTIVITY

- In what area or areas of your life do you get most overwhelmed?
- What fears are buried beneath that overwhelm?
- Take a moment and re-word those fears/beliefs so that they are not only more in line with the truth but are also more powerfully able to move you a step closer to your goals.

TEN

I Assume

"Do not let your assumptions about a culture block your
ability to perceive the individual, or you will fail."
—*Brandon Sanderson*

Two additional unhealthy habits likely to don your
doorstep right behind your fear of just about
everything and all of your mindset issues around
money are perception and assumption. Yes, others' perception of you (or your perception of their perception, which—for the record—is usually wrong) will likely enter your mind now and again (if not every thirteen seconds),

but that's not the perception of which I speak. Think about the perceptions you have and the assumptions you make about other entrepreneurs' levels of success. About their levels of happiness. About the size of their bank accounts. We make assumptions all the time that are not only likely wildly incorrect, they're dangerous.

We assume that those who appear to have "made it" in any field are living the good life at all times. We assume they are serene and happy in their high-priced yoga attire and silk PJs. We assume they love driving their brand new Tesla, vacationing wherever and whenever they want, and enjoying constantly satisfying relationships with their loved ones.

I remember when I first heard the news of Robin Williams' passing. I was utterly confused. Saddened also, of course, but the main emotion I remember feeling was confusion. Robin Williams? The guy who was notorious for being optimistic and funny and goofy? The guy who appeared to love life to the fullest each and every day? The guy who had an incredible career, family, friends, and financial security—*that* Robin Williams just took his own life?

And then, several years later, the news broke that Chester Bennington had also died from suicide. This news hit me differently because I'd briefly—very briefly—met Chester and his wife, Talinda, a year or two earlier at an event in Scottsdale.

Let's rewind, shall we?

I'm a huge fan of *Million Dollar Listing New York.* Huge fan is probably an understatement. I want to be best friends forever with Fredrik, find a guy like Ryan who finally took his head out of his ass and married Emilia, and spend a weekend with the contagious energy of Luis Ortiz. I love people with good energy, period, and Luis is in my Top 5 list of people I've known (or known of) who appear to have it.

Anyway, I was driving home from meetings one day and somehow heard that Luis was in town for a realtor-related event. After I pulled over so as to prevent a crash, I called my friend, Shane, who is good friends with two amazing women in Scottsdale, one of whom is a highly skilled luxury realtor and the other an incredible luxury event planner. Yes, Monica and Angelica, I'm talking about you. You never thought after the night I'm about to describe that you'd end up in a book one day, did you? Ah the many things we have no idea will ever happen. Anyway, at this point, I only knew of Monica, so I jokingly said on Shane's voice mail, "You know how I feel about Luis Ortiz, and he's in town for a realtor event. Can Monica get me in on this?"

An hour or so later, I noticed I had three missed calls and one voicemail from Shane.

"Elizabeth, you're going to need to call me back right now. I can have you sitting at Luis's table at tonight's event if you want to go."

I saw black. I seriously think I lost consciousness for a moment.

As I called Shane back (my fingers would not dial fast enough), I said aloud to absolutely no one, "I have positively nothing to wear to something like this!" Shane answered and communicated that one of the *Million Dollar Listing LA* guys was supposed to be at Monica's table—along with Luis—but had to cancel last-minute, so they had an opening.

You see, I had called Shane in the first place thinking that the likelihood of this actually becoming a reality was somewhere between zero percent and zero percent. I wasn't even realistically inquiring. It was really just a "You know how I feel about this person and he's in town!" type of inquiry, in much the same way that I would, a few years later, take great joy in the fact that a kind air traffic controller at a private local airport "winked" confirmation that Adam Levine might have, in fact, landed there at some point. (Why that's confidential, I haven't the slightest idea. It's an airport, not a strip club, but I still felt very cool to be in-the-know.)

"You are going to let clothing stop you?" he said incredulously. "I'll call Monica; she'll let you 'shop' in her closet."

I could not go shop in her closet. I'd never met her and I'd act like an idiot and she'd ban me from the event.

"Fine. I'll go to TJ Maxx. Pray for me; I love that place, but they never have anything when I actually need something!"

The next three hours were a blur. I got a dress (come to think of it, where is that dress?) and heels, and after running a flat iron through my hair more times than Jamie, my Hair Guru, would approve of, I drove an hour east to the resort where the event was taking place. I'm going to talk more about this event and what I learned from it in a moment, but for now, I'd like to focus on Chester Bennington. Chester and Talinda had a personal connection to the hospital that hosts the Stars of the Season gala, and not only were they at the event but Linkin Park would be performing outside on the patio afterward.

I remember when Chester and his wife approached our table. I thought, "He's so much shorter than I imagined!" He was the most kind, gracious, humble man. I quite literally could not take my eyes off of his wife. I wanted to say, "I know you aren't airbrushed right now, but what products are you using because ohmigod." She's not only gorgeous, she has incredible grace. A few words were exchanged between our table and this husband/wife powerhouse, and that was that.

Until he popped up on stage and took on a completely different persona. And that was the moment I fell in love with Chester Bennington.

In private, he was a quiet, humble, kind man. And yet when he took the stage, the artist came out and, well, if you've seen him perform, you know what I mean. It's incredible. So when the news came that he'd taken his life, I was sad and confused. Profoundly confused.

Again, he seemed to "have it all." He was doing what he loved, making plenty of money doing it, married to an amazing woman he loved and vice versa, blessed with great kids, admired and respected, and had philanthropic causes about which he was passionate. What compels a person like that to end his life?

I was equally shocked when Anthony Bourdain took his life. And Kate Spade. And then, recently, my very own Luis Ortiz went public with his debilitating suicidal thoughts. Luis—my high-energy, everything-is-beautiful lover of life. Luis, who I sat across from at the table as he bid an unbelievable amount of money to get on stage for 90 seconds with Linkin Park after the gala. Find the YouTube video of his performance. Just search "Luis Ortiz Linkin Park rap." He's incredible. He freestyle rapped an entire verse in *Spanish*. I looked at him on that stage, having learned of his journey going from working as a janitor when he first arrived in NYC to finding incredible success as a realtor and, at that moment, brilliantly rapping in another language alongside Chester Bennington—an opportunity he got by donating a generous amount of money to a children's hospital. In that moment, I closed my eyes and reminded myself that Anything is Possible.

All this to say, we have no idea what is really going on in someone's mind behind the curtain. Just because someone appears to have it all, be it all, be happy, feel confident, and radiate optimism doesn't mean that he or she is in that state at all times. So when we compare ourselves to others, we have to be careful about what we're comparing ourselves to and acknowledge the fact that we don't actually know what we're comparing ourselves to. We're comparing ourselves to the ideas we have about someone else's existence.

People make a few assumptions about me with frequency. "I want to be you when I grow up" is a statement I've heard several times, and it often leaves me puzzled. What about me do people want to be? Because it can't possibly have anything to do with my hypochondriac tendencies, the level of anxiety I battle, or my age spots.

One day not long ago, my own sister said to me, "You're fearless."

And I responded, "You're insane."

Truth: I'm terrified. All the time.

I'm nothing that even resembles fearless. I have simply forced myself to push through fear over the years. I stare it in the face and try to figure out where it comes from, and in doing so, challenge myself to push past it. But I have moments almost every single day wherein I'm afraid of failing, of disappointing people, of being invisible, of not being of value, of being rejected, and of being out of Sumatra K-Cups.

Sometimes when I drive through Starbucks, I put on a smile and up my energy just to say, "Good morning!" and "Thank you!" to the barista who's handing my coffee out the window simply because I know (since my oldest daughter, Grace, works there) that ninety-seven percent of customers are either in a bad mood or flat-out rude. Therefore, even when I'm ready to cry, I put on a happy face just before approaching and as I'm pulling away from that window. What they are left with is the notion that I "have the best energy." But ain't nobody coming out to comfort the hysterical lady parked haphazardly in the parking lot guzzling her iced latte like a lunatic. In their minds, that lady doesn't exist.

What I've learned is that the only person worth comparing myself to is myself. I can only strive to be better than I was yesterday (or an hour ago). If I'm constantly comparing myself to someone else, about whom I only know a small bit, the goal post for my own happiness and satisfaction with myself will be constantly moving. I don't like moving targets. It's one of eighteen reasons I don't hunt.

What we often come to discover is that our perception does not necessarily match another person's reality. We assume that they get to live their life a certain way, and we then base our personal expectations on that assumption. When we expect to become something we don't even fully understand, how on earth do we expect to purposefully get there?

As of this writing, the brilliant Sarah Centrella cannot smell or taste anything as a result of a bad cold she contracted earlier this year. It is my great hope that, as you're reading this, the doctors have figured out how to get her taste and smell intact. But, while everyone sits around and thinks, "Sarah's life is so incredibly amazing from top to bottom" (and I think she'd agree that it truly is amazing), the woman cannot smell or taste coffee. Please ponder that for a moment and then send some good energy into the universe so that these senses can be returned to her, pronto.

Vision is one thing; expectation is another. However, it's nearly impossible, it seems, to get away from the idea of expectations because having them is so ingrained in us from a young age. Our parents have expectations of us; our friends have expectations of us; society has expectations of us. And, in turn, we have expectations of people and situations. When we embark on something, we expect it to work out a certain way. But we must differentiate between vision and expectation.

Both vision and hope are open to modification. Expectation is more rigid. We expect a certain feeling, a certain describable outcome. And when those don't come to pass as expected, we are disappointed. Or pissed.

Think about how the word "expect" is often used as we're growing up: "I expect you to finish your homework." "I expect you to finish your dinner." "I expect you to be kind to your sister." But what does that look like? If, in the eyes of a parent, "Be kind to your sister" includes painting her toenails while telling her she's the most fantastic sister ever, and in your eyes, it simply includes saying, "You look nice today," the expectation hasn't been met in the eye of the parent. The biggest challenge comes from the fact that expectations are rarely clearly defined (if they're defined at all). When someone's expectation of us isn't clarified, we perceive it the way that we do, and when the two don't match up, someone's getting grounded.

Expectations are actually quite dangerous. We see something unfold in a certain way (even if we don't know it), and when it doesn't unfold in that exact way we believe something (or someone) has failed. This reality is especially perilous in our personal lives. If our friend or life partner has no idea what our expectation is or what it looks like, they're almost guaranteed to miss the mark on some level. For some reason, we are cautious to outright tell people what our expectations are because we think, "You should know." Sometimes, that's true. Other times, it's really not.

Professionally speaking, at the most foundational level we expect to succeed. The challenge is that we don't clarify for ourselves what that success looks like! To simply say, "I want to be making millions of dollars" or "I want the business to be successful" is nowhere near clear enough. We have to get extremely clear on what we *hope* will happen and what our *vision* is while being willing to *assume* that we're already there. The space between what we can physically see as proof that our ideal outcome exists and what we assume is out there energetically but not yet visible in front of us is where faith and trust come in so that we can pivot as necessary in order to reach the end goal. The target is end goal, not the method by which we get there.

Your journey is not going to be like anyone else's. And that's okay! That doesn't mean that any part of your journey is right and theirs is wrong or theirs is right and yours is wrong. They are simply different. As long as you are in alignment with your goals and values at all times, your steps are just that—*your steps* on a unique journey.

Let's talk a bit more about assumption for a moment because, frankly, it gets a really bad rap. To be fair, assuming anything about anyone else is rarely productive, but assumption, as a concept, can actually have an incredibly positive affect when we do it with regard to ourselves.

The Law of Assumption is as real a universal principle as is the Law of Attraction (or any of the other universal laws out there). First posited by Neville Goddard in 1969, this law can be both the hardest and the most fun to grow skilled at. One of the hardest things to do sometimes is "act as if"—to assume that the reality we're striving toward is already ours despite the physical evidence to the contrary. The universe truly doesn't know what exists and what doesn't in material form. If we say it exists, it exists. So, we have to assume that we're already there. We have to assume that we're living our ideal life, that we have enough—that we *are* enough—*before* physical evidence proves that as fact.

You've undoubtedly heard the phrase "perception is reality." When we perceive or assume that someone is unkind, we will attach unkind meaning to every word they say or every facial expression they make. We will literally assume into existence the reality that we need to be true to support our belief. The opposite also holds true. If we assume that people are kind, if we perceive people's actions as supportive and helpful, that's what we'll see more of.

The key is to assume our ideal outcome, regardless of whether or not we yet have physical evidence of its existence. My ideal outcome includes the following: my bank account is full, my body is toned and fit, my business is growing faster and is more satisfying day-to-day than I ever imagined, I have a circle of incredible friends, I'm thrilled to finally have an industrial condo downtown, and I'm excited to jet off to Maui next month (and yes, I'm flying first-class). Physical evidence proves *some* of that ideal outcome but not all of it (yet). However, by assuming the reality anyway, I begin to live as if it's already true. The reason my bank account is full is that I work hard, intentionally and consistently. My body is toned and fit because I work out regularly and eat clean. Because I have a circle of incredible friends (and I do), I don't tolerate bullshit from idiots. Because I'm heading to Maui next month, I have to stick with my daily and weekly goals even when I don't feel like it so that when I jet off on that trip I can set work aside and really enjoy it. As far as the universe is concerned, all of this assumption is already reality. It may not be a reality I can see today, but it exists. And it's only a matter of time before it shows up in a tangible way.

The Stars of the Season gala was full of unexpected lessons. I was basically on my own in an enormous venue with extraordinarily successful people (who I'm quite certain did not purchase their dresses that day or from T.J.

Maxx). Monica, Angelica, and their husbands were as gracious as could be, but let's be real, they had a lot of people vying for their attention, and they were responsible for Luis, so babysitting me wasn't at the top of their list.

Therefore, I had to do some assuming of my own.

I had to assume that this was not the first time I'd been to an event like this (even though it was). I had to assume that I wasn't beyond uncomfortable in my heels (was I ever). I had to assume that this was just a normal Saturday night for me, comfortably weaving in and out of people wearing more diamonds and with more luxurious hair than I'd ever seen up close and personal. I had to remind myself that no one knew I was as uncomfortable as I was except me.

Interestingly, almost any time I made eye contact with someone (which wasn't hard to do because people were everywhere), a conversation would start. I'd genuinely compliment someone's dress at the dessert table because obviously that's where I felt most at home, or someone would make a comment to me about how something looked too good to eat, at which point I'd look at them incredulously and counter with, "It looks too good *not* to eat!" A nice conversation then commenced.

I assumed the sense of comfortable confidence I aspired to have. And I had the most incredible time. No one in the venue was looking to prove anything to anyone, which was great because, if they were, it could have turned into a highly competitive (and obnoxious) pissing contest. I did not talk to a single person who didn't have an authentic energy about them. And that's something money can't buy. You can buy an expensive dress and Jimmy Choo heels and a blow-out and diamond-studded cufflinks. But you can't buy stunning energy and authenticity.

TIME TO TAKE ACTION

JOURNAL ACTIVITY

- Take a moment to consider the assumptions you often make about others in both your professional and personal life.
- With regard to those that are negative in any way or elicit negative feelings, *what if those weren't true?* What would that change?
- Now think about what assumptions you'd like to make going forward that are intentionally in line with where you are going.

ELEVEN

It's Just a Bad Habit

"The second half of a man's life is made up of nothing but
the habits he has acquired during the first half."
—*Fyodor Dostoevsky*

Whether you're 23, 33, 43, or 83, you have a large number of years in the arsenal during which you've created certain habits. These habits have, in fact, become your lifestyle because you've been doing them—consciously or unconsciously—for so long. They either serve you or they don't. In all likelihood, if there is any area of your life you'd like to move forward, there is at least one habit that's derailing you. You think it's serving you. You often convince yourself that it's serving you in order to justify it because getting rid of it sounds hard and boring and *Ohmigod what will I do without my Real Housewives?* But it's not serving you, plain and simple.

Busy is not the same as productive. Not by a long shot. I constantly hear the phrase, "I just don't have time." Or "When exactly would I do that?" We've convinced ourselves that we are crunched for time, but in reality, we are completely deluding ourselves with regard to the habits through which we are spending our time.

People who say they don't have $37 for a workshop are dropping $8 a day at Starbucks. People who say they don't have time to write for thirty minutes a day are binge-watching *13 Reasons Why* in the evening. People who are busy actually being productive don't talk about how busy they are. When you ask them how things are going, they don't groan and say, "Ohmigod it's just so much."

Just as busy does not equal productive, motion does not equal progress.

Do you grasp the concept of physics? Me either. Nevertheless, Newton's first law states that every object will remain in motion in a straight line unless compelled to change its state by the action of an external force. Do you know what that force is when it comes to getting your business to the next level or your book started?

Overthinking.

You daydream about the products you'll create and the stories you'll tell and the high-level concepts of your outline and the feeling of standing on stage with all eyes excitedly fixed on you and your increased authority as a personal brand and traveling with your partner or family as a result of your business growth.

And yes, that dreaming is motion—in the sense that you're *doing* something—but you aren't making any *progress*. The needle isn't moving. You've visualized what your life looks like after your company is established or your book is published, but visualization and realization are two different states. Your visualization has to be strong enough to motivate you to take a powerful step each and every day toward your goal. It doesn't have to be a massive step. You don't have to figure out a way to hurl yourself over a fifteen-foot crevasse that's 32,000 feet in the air. That may seem a powerful and courageous leap, but if you miss, you'll actually set yourself back (and incur a pretty nasty hospital bill).

SHORTCUT TO ENOUGH

VISION + INTENTIONAL, CONSISTENT ACTION = RESULTS

I haven't believed in the concept of New Year's Resolutions in a long, long time. One thing I know to be true about myself (and that likely won't surprise you by this point) is that I tend to get really excited about something, launch into it at 100mph and then fizzle out, totally and utterly exhausted and defeated within ninety-six hours. It's happened so many times that it's a full-fledged, undeniable pattern.

I switched over to the concept of New Year's Goals about a decade ago. The challenge with this approach was that the goals were only stated. There was no *how* put in place in order to get me there. There was no action step between "This is my goal" and "It's December 31; why the hell haven't I met the goal?" It's great to say, "I want to find more joy this year" or "I want to better my health this year" or "I want to make half a million dollars this year." But, if you don't lay out a plan to inch closer and closer to that goal each and every day, it ain't gonna happen without the assistance of a miracle. And if your mindset isn't right, a miracle probably won't occur either. More on that later.

Plans aren't my thing. Have a mentioned that? I rarely make shopping lists. I almost never make weekly meal plans. I have never in my life written a business plan. I think I see those activities as getting in the way of the end result, as time wasted. They're planning, not *doing*. I'm a doer. I'm an action taker. Just jump in there and get it done. That's how I've always approached tasks, and frankly, I've been complimented on it my entire life as though it were admirable, which did not help me to see how flawed an approach it actually was. I mean, I guess it's admirable to be willing to jump off the cliff and grow wings on the way down, and being an action taker is awesome and not something I'm ever going to stop being. But, as Kirk said, "I'd rather know just a little bit about the cliff I'm jumping from, how far down it is, and what the wind speeds are."

The result of this total and complete unwillingness to plan is often some version of that moment when Cici is scanning the very last item on the belt at Target and I recognize that I don't have the *one thing* I came in there for to begin with (toothpaste, remember?). I shout, "OH SHIT, I KNEW I forgot something!" (I proceed to do the exact same thing the next week, by the way, because it's too time-consuming to put in place a preventative measure before then. There are too many other things on the to-do list.)

Sometimes, you reach the point where you simply have no other choice but to admit that something has to change. My best friend and Spiritual Guru, Erin, calls this "reaching your bottom." I occasionally call her and say, "Welp, I made this mistake again," and she'll say, "That's okay. You simply haven't hit your bottom yet." This is always a scary moment as I wonder just how bad my personal bottom is going to look!

The conversation I mentioned that I'd had with Kirk, the one wherein he told me he was seriously concerned for my business longevity, was a huge catalyst in finally compelling me to curl up and rest my head on the cold earth at the bottom of my own very (very) deep hole. Not long after, someone I'd been following on social media opened up a group coaching program, and I said (with nary a plan in terms of how I'd pay for it, of course), "I'm in!" It had been a while since I'd been part of a formal group and had a coach or mentor holding me accountable day after day, week after week. It was time to get back into that world.

This particular coach was Tommy Baker (the same Tommy Baker who was gracious enough to write the Foreword to this book), and I'm not going to give away too many of his practices because he spent years learning and honing them. Also, I'm not interested in an intellectual property lawsuit this year. But trust me, if you want accountability and are willing to get *real* honest with yourself in every area of your life, you want to get a coach. You don't want to *need* to, you want to *want* to.

With that said, one of the first things participants had to do was embark on a daily ritual of six habits. Tommy calls it the Daily Six.

This daily ritual is comprised of a non-negotiable set of—you guessed it—six tasks that must be completed—you guessed it—daily. Preferably, they are completed in the morning, and as such, they create your morning routine. Morning routines are a topic in and of themselves, and when you begin to pay attention, you realize that all the great entrepreneurs and creators in this world have a morning routine. It made me fairly nervous to begin recognizing that my morning routine—the one I had employed for the previous eighteen years—is pretty unacceptable. For the record, it looked like this:

- Wake up exhausted.
- Lie in bed and dread all that's to come.
- Scroll through Facebook and Instagram while the kids get ready.
- Listen to everyone argue as they make lunches and complain about how small the kitchen is.
- Drive kids to school.
- Call Karen and talk for an hour.
- Make coffee.
- Pace.
- Daydream about what it will be like when I have a modern, industrial condo in downtown Phoenix with floor-to-ceiling windows.
- Research modern, industrial condos in downtown Phoenix with floor-to-ceiling windows.
- Research cool collars for the Great Dane I don't yet have (and have no space *to* have).
- Check email and social media. Twice.
- Stare at the wall for between nine and fourteen minutes.
- Decide I want to paint the wall a different color.
- Get on Houzz to identify new color.
- Exit Houzz (four hours later) to start working.

No, I wasn't confident that was the kind of morning routine Tony Robbins, Tim Ferriss, or Nicole Montez employs. But it was what I'd done since forever, and it was where my comfort zone had made a happy home.

Anyway, my new morning routine was to consist of (in no particular order): gratitude, encouragement, meditation, fitness, study, and purpose. If incorporating six new tasks into one's day was proving too overwhelming, it was advised that we start with three and increase from there. The fact is, if you bite off more than you can chew, you're going to choke. But I'm a masochistic overachiever so I went for all six from the get-go.

GRATITUDE wasn't a problem. I can rattle off twenty people, places, events, or realities for which I'm grateful anytime, anywhere.

ENCOURAGEMENT wasn't new for me either, but I found that I really enjoyed (far more than I thought I would) identifying someone in my inner circle, outer circle, or periphery whom I could call, text, Facebook message, or email with some encouragement and a message of how thankful I was to work with them, have worked with them, have them in my life, have learned from them, be their mother, etc.

Then we got to the more nightmarish tasks, in ascending order of difficulty.

STUDY requires that you do something I love to do: read (or listen to a podcast or watch a TED Talk or something of that ilk). Basically, it requires that you consume knowledge and/or a new perspective. It allows you to increase your mental and/or spiritual and/or emotional state by one percent. What I found most challenging about it was justifying carving out five to thirty minutes to read when I needed to be doing eight zillion other things. It was suggested that I start with just five pages before getting out of bed and work up from there. Done.

Tommy's a smart guy, so he didn't leave us to our own devices when it came to selecting a book. He asked what each of us was specifically struggling with. For me, it's distractions.

The next morning a package arrived from Amazon, and it felt like Christmas. First of all, it was nearly Christmas when this happened. Second of all, I had no idea what was in the package. I knew it was a book, but I didn't know what book could possibly help me understand the value of getting rid of distractions (not to mention how to do it).

Deep Work by Cal Newport was the perfect choice, and consuming its wisdom became my obsession. From it, I noted three or four other books I wanted to read right afterward. The greatest lesson I learned in devouring this book didn't come from the book's contents (which are, in and of themselves, invaluable). What I learned was that knowing you want something is 49 percent of the battle. The other 51 percent comes from a combined 35 percent understanding how that "something" can benefit you and how you're going to get there plus 14 percent learning how not to cling as tightly as a one-year-old to his parent's leg to the intricate details of the how. (I'll discuss that last part in detail toward the end. It's critical, and I wouldn't leave you without a thorough understanding of what the hell I'm talking about here, don't you worry.) *Deep Work* gave me so much insight into how deep focus serves the world's greatest creators and how we're all getting sidetracked by surface-level time sucks such as social media, reality TV, and water-cooler gossip and drama. It put science (one that I could understand, anyway) behind its rules. It made sense.

The PURPOSE segment of our day was to be focused on one and only one thing we were going to do each day in the area of our passion. For most of us, that was the area of our entrepreneurial venture. Some of us worked full- or part-time in other areas to pay the bills while we built our dream businesses. Some of us already had a great position at a great company and wanted to climb higher. Therefore, carving out time and making sure that time was well-spent was critical. You have to actually *move the needle* every single day, not just sit and think about how great it's going to be to have your own jet with a hot pilot.

Interestingly, many days during that time period my purpose task involved writing this book! Before I began including study in my daily routine, I was often hard-pressed to identify what to write about each day. I had aggressive word count goals, and they needed to have a point. Simply writing "I've got nothing" over and over again until I hit my daily word count goal does not a valuable book create.

My creative spark was ignited almost every morning simply by the book I read or the podcast I listened to. A point would be made that would jog my memory and I'd immediately jot down an epiphany on a Post-It Note, and that thought often ended up being the focal point for my writing that day.

MEDITATION. Kill me. Seriously. Every day? For at least seven minutes? Just the thought of it—even sometimes still—makes me want to turn on some really bad TV and pretend that this directive does not exist. Ironically, the tasks to which we are most resistant are the ones we most need to lean into. It's the only way to build new habits and, as a result, re-wire our brains. Honestly, I got so irritated with people who would say, "I had the greatest forty-five-minute meditation today. I felt so clear and peaceful." Tommy's response: "That's so powerful!" My response: "I hate your guts."

What I had to (and have to) continually remind myself is that I'm not in competition with those who have mastered the art of meditating (or seem as though they have). I'm competing with myself. My goal is to be one percent more relaxed and focused every day than I was the day before, to take one more breath without thinking about everything I have to do than I did the day before. Some days, that definitely doesn't happen. And then I look at the words Begin Again tattooed on my arm, and I vow to do that (the next day).

FITNESS is the final category, and it's the hardest one for me. It's even harder than meditation because it requires that I actually move and possibly sweat. I talked in *You Cannot Be Serious* about my fitness pursuits over the years, so if you read that book you have the foundation to know where I'm coming from.

I've never been particularly athletic. I've tried—but for mostly the wrong reasons (usually meaning, "That boy is super cute, and he's an athlete. I'm totally taking up field hockey this year.") My junior year in high school, my boyfriend was a star athlete. He was one of the state's best swimmers and soccer players. I always felt less-than when surrounded by the female swimmers and field hockey players he got to spend his afternoons practicing with or on the field next to. So I decided I'd join a sports team. I decided to run cross-country (this was just after I quit tennis, in case you're mentally managing a timeline).

Honest to God, I have no idea what I was thinking. I still remember the first day of practice. We emerged from the school as a group of about twenty for a two-mile run for which I was beyond wildly unprepared. I think I'd run, at most, an eighth of a mile before. Over two separate evenings.

I made sure I was in the front of the pack coming out of the high school double doors. I really wanted to impress him. I even bought neon orange running shorts because they looked great against my tan legs. He did not so much as glance in my direction. By the time I got back to the school seven or eight hours later, I was dead last and almost dead period. At that point, he *was* looking because the entire soccer team was wondering if an ambulance needed to be called. Plus, my neon shorts were suddenly acting as a beacon against the setting son.

But I kept with it, dammit. There was the day my friend Catie was literally pulling me up Route 896 in Newark, Delaware to finish our run. It was probably about a week later when I said, "You guys, I've suffered a major knee injury, and as much as I want to keep doing this, I simply can't. Doctor's orders." That doctor was a fictitious character, and he's still one of my favorite practitioners to date.

A few years ago, I caved to the peer pressure of a group of amazingly fun moms at my kids' school and agreed to do CrossFit with them three times per week. I got the gym's decal for the back window of my car and everything. On Day One, their head trainer, Kelly, told me that if I threw up she'd give me a free tank top. My friend (also named Kelly) took pity on me after I got excited about the tank top and bought one for me instead. *Breathe Later*, it said. Cool. Will do.

It. Was. Awful. Now, even though I finished last every single day I still finished, and I'm here to profess that I was in the best shape of my life after three months. But, at that point, it was May in Phoenix and the gym had no air conditioning and just...no. Once you lose momentum, however, restarting is extremely difficult. That fall I moved on to P90X, Insanity, and Piyo, all of which required self-accountability (meaning that I lasted two days, maybe three). I then signed up for Pilates (which did last a while because I loved the girls I went with and was charged an extra $25 if I bailed within twelve hours of the class I'd signed up for).

For the first month or so of Tommy's Daily Six routine, I struggled. Badly. Truth be told, some days I still struggle! But before long I began to connect the routine to my overall growth, and that connection was more addictive than anything else—even *Billions, Power,* or *Homeland.* In the beginning, each time I got to the meditation or fitness portion of the Daily Six, I cussed Tommy out (in my head). But then I did it. I didn't force myself to meditate for thirty minutes every day nor did I expect myself to run two miles or do a sixty-minute Tabata workout. I just did *something.*

This is why, when working with clients, I say "Write *something!*" Daily word count goals are important and can be helpful, but if you have a bad day (and we all do) the directive isn't "2,500 words or nothing." If you write only ten words, you're ten words further ahead than you were the day before. You've moved the needle.

The oldest example in the book (that I can think of anyway) is throwing change into a jar. Seventeen cents here, twelve cents there, and before you know it, you go pour all that money into the fun machine and it spits out $156. If you only improve or increase by one percent per day, that's a 36.5 percent increase over the course of a year. You'll be over three times further ahead in a year doing only one percent extra per day. The compound effect of not stopping is remarkable. And it will change your life.

Every night before going to bed, I identify the one task that *has* to get done the next day. Sometimes it's a task that will take several hours, sometimes it's not. But it's the one thing that moves the needle for my business. I tackle that task first as often as possible. That way, no matter what chaos ensues during the rest of the day, I've accomplished that one thing. I then list out the three or four next most important tasks. I review these lists in the morning after I express gratitude, provide encouragement, and practice (sometimes struggle through) meditation. I'm clear on my day so that I run it; it doesn't run me.

Establishing new habits isn't about resentfully checking things off a to-do list. In the beginning, that's very much what it will feel like, for sure. But the longer you do them, the more you will connect them with your overall progress. Your brain will be re-wired to *compel* you to do these things each and every day. Your day won't feel complete without them. In turn, your personal and professional growth will continue to increase. That cycle is addictive—and it's a great addiction to have!

TIME TO TAKE ACTION

JOURNAL ACTIVITY

- What are your habits that are not serving you professionally?
- What are your habits that are not serving you personally?
- What is ONE way you're willing to begin replacing an old, unproductive habit with a new one every single day?

TWELVE

I'm an Idiot

"Don't trade your authenticity for approval."
—*Unknown*

We all have both cheerleaders and naysayers in our heads. The challenge is to enable the cheerleaders to out-scream the naysayers. Imagine if, every time you made a mistake, your inner cheerleader said, "It's okay! You're doing great!" That's rarely what happens. Instead, we hear, "You idiot." If you're like me, your inner cheerleader says it out loud.

My oldest daughter and I have a joke between us where we say, "You're doing great, sweetie." We don't say this to each other. We say it when we see someone clearly trying too hard at something he or she clearly doesn't want to be doing. But imagine if our inner cheerleader said that when we made a mistake—even sarcastically! It's far better than what we typically hear.

"What am I doing?"

"Get it together, Liz."

"I'm losing it."

"I'm overwhelmed and terrified."

"I have no idea what I was thinking."

The list goes on.

I'm 97 percent there. Maybe 98 percent," I told my new coach one morning. You'd think that would be enough (pun intended). But it isn't. Because until you're 100 percent in, 100 percent convicted in who you are, what you do, who you do it for, what you charge, and what you *don't* do, the universe will hold out on you.

I was swiftly reminded, "The universe is waiting on that two to three percent. It doesn't fuck around. It doesn't show up for someone who's 97 percent there. Or 98 percent. Or 99 percent. Think of it this way: is it ideal if your partner is 97 percent faithful? Or if your drinking water doesn't have lead in it 98 percent of the time? Or your kid escapes bullying 99 percent of the time?" Thank you, Julian. Point taken.

But figuring out that extra two to three percent is the hardest. It's the final hurdle. The hurdle over which most people never jump because they're too afraid, and therefore convince themselves that 97 percent is pretty damn good and better than most.

That's what I did for a long time.

To be clear, this isn't about being 100 percent perfect. No such state exists. It's about being 100 percent sure of who you are, 100 percent aware of the limiting beliefs that are holding you back even if you're still working on them, 100 percent in acknowledgment of the negative self-talk that has become so habitual that you don't even realize that you're outright telling the universe, "Don't give me what I want. I'm not ready yet."

We all find ourselves in moments when we feel like we aren't enough. We feel like we aren't successful enough or toned enough or motivated enough or determined enough or wealthy enough or sensitive enough or emotional enough or sexy enough or athletic enough or thoughtful enough or badass enough.

Why don't we stop to consider that, in all likelihood, the *enough* by which we are judging ourselves has absolutely nothing to do with us! The guy who suddenly left you for a younger woman? That had nothing to do with you. The woman who wasn't honest about her misunderstanding of the difference between separated and divorced? Same principle applies. The job you didn't get because you "aren't smart enough?" Would it surprise you to learn that the executive team actually thinks you're too smart, and they're afraid you're going to leave the minute you get a better offer? (And, let's face it, you are— because you're smart enough to do so!) Or, perhaps you *are* smart enough, just not in that competency area, and in the end, you would have hated the position so they actually did you a huge favor.

We have no idea what truly goes on in the minds of others, but somehow we continue to make others' decisions about us reflect our innate belief that we aren't [fill in the blank] enough. WHY DO WE DO THAT? I'll tell you why: we're not yet in a space where we believe that we are enough just as we are. We aren't the best fit for everyone or every position. But that has nothing to do with being enough. They are unconditionally mutually exclusive concepts.

Think about it this way. Have you heard the story about the dog and the elephant in the animal sanctuary who are the very best of friends? In any other area of life, dogs typically aren't "enough" for elephants, nor are elephants "enough" for dogs. But in this case, for whatever reason, they just fit. Now, what would happen if every dog believed that she isn't enough because she doesn't have an elephant for a best friend? Remember, "Everybody is a genius. But if you judge a fish by its ability to climb a tree, it will spend its entire life believing it is stupid."

The fish needs to realize and accept that it's a fish, and as such, it can't climb a tree. It needs to focus on what it *can* do well. It needs to swim with the current, not against it (see what I did there?). It can spend its life trying to climb a tree, but only if that's what the fish himself really wants. If he's only doing it to prove the naysayers wrong, it's a waste of his life based entirely on misguided motivations.

I recognize that mindset work is all the rage, but there's a reason it's been trendy for so long that it's not even appropriate to call it a trend any longer. It works. And the majority of us need it. We need to know not just what our worth is but that we *are* worth. Like most other life-altering approaches, however, mindset work employed in a vacuum isn't impactful, just as the Law of Attraction doesn't work if you simply sit on your couch all day in sweatpants visualizing in great detail millions of dollars and a baby zebra showing up on your front porch. Simply visualizing and waiting won't manifest the outcome you dream about.

You know what's really frightening? Paying attention to the way we talk to ourselves. I mean, if I talked to my friends the way I talk to myself much of the time, I would have zero friends. "What am I doing?" "I'm never going to get this right." "This is never going to work." "Where did that wrinkle come from?" "I swear these pants fit yesterday. Why am I disgusting?" People, this has to stop. *Saturday Night Live's* Stuart Smalley had the right idea with his daily affirmation: "I'm good enough, I'm smart enough, and doggone it people like me." It's about time we all followed suit.

Ego is a wonderful, powerful, horrible thing. Some would argue that it doesn't exist at all. For the purposes of this book, which is not based in principles of existential philosophy, let's consider ego as pride. It's the part of you that wants to feel smart, feel like you're contributing, feel like others value you, not feel stupid, not have to say, "I don't know," not be embarrassed, not feel small.

I like to say, "Le'go the Ego," and in this context, you have to mispronounce ego so that the construction properly rhymes. I don't like mispronunciations. Ever. Unless they are intentional. In fact, I know things are clicking with my clients when I can say to them simply, "Le'go the Eggo" and they immediately know to what I'm referring, not directing them to put down their toaster waffle.

None of us wants to feel small. Some of us go too far in the other direction in order not to (often referred to as peacocking). But when we really start to pay attention to ourselves, it becomes easier and easier to recognize when our ego is taking over—it's usually the moment when we start to spiral into an explanation or justification that keeps getting muddier and muddier because, in the end, we are looking only to "win" or successfully defend our position.

It's not about winning. It's not about being the best. It's not about being better than anyone other than the person you were yesterday. It's not about proving yourself to anyone except yourself. Once you adopt an attitude of Going for Growth, allow yourself to be human, accept your own limitations (we all have them), and adopt boundaries (that you actually enforce), everything flows with much greater ease.

We worry that people will judge our opinion so we stay silent. We worry that our prices are too high so we lower them. And lower them again. And again. Until we find ourselves face-to-face with Day 214. (Newsflash: it's as easy and hard to sell a $25,000 coaching program as it is to sell a $25 mini-course.) Our ego is trying to protect us the same way it did in the caveman days. It says, "Danger! Run!" and we do. But we aren't running from a hungry bear. We're running from public scrutiny. Which, for some reason, seems to be scarier much of the time. Newsflash Number Two: no one's message is unique anymore. It's simply delivered in a unique package that a certain tribe identifies with. Find your tribe. Serve them. Nurture them. Connect with them. Trust me, everyone else is doing just fine without you.

So many of us in the entrepreneur space have trouble believing that we are worth our own price of admission. Whether we have a physical product or service to offer, we love talking about what problem we solve, but the moment someone asks, "How much is it?" we panic. We worry, "Are they going to think I'm crazy to be asking for this much money? Will they laugh behind my back as they're walking away?"

Once you get to a point where you can announce your products with confidence, everything changes. Too often, we think we aren't worth others' financial and time investments because we don't have the right letters after our name, we don't have the proper official credentials. I don't know a single attorney who has a problem charging

$300 per hour for her time because, if for no other reason, she's got the degree and the marketplace says that her hourly rate is in line with the competition. I also have yet to meet an attorney who provides me with $300 per hour's worth of value, but perhaps I'm not looking in the right places.

Attorneys don't necessarily know their worth. The industry tells them what it is, and they go along for the ride. For those of us running our own businesses, especially service-based businesses, assessing our worth can be challenging at first. But if you don't know your own worth, how can you expect anyone else to know it (and pay for it)? The fact of the matter is that a product or service's value is whatever the market will pay. We've all seen products and services we know are wildly underpriced, and we've seen even more products and services that are wildly *over*priced!

Worth versus value. There is a clear difference between the two (although, until you understand it, the difference can be blurry). To increase your worth (in terms of how much you're paid), you have to increase your value in the eyes of your customers.

The key is finding the sweet spot. In the jewelry space, I used to spend a lot of time listening to Megan Auman, a fantastic designer and incredible business woman. She had a pair of earrings that required $5 worth of materials to produce. But she sold them for $100+ over and over and over again. That's what the market was willing to pay for them. We see coaches put together courses and sell them for $997 because that's the "going rate" for such courses and occasionally find them only to be worth a quarter of that. Sometimes, they end up being worth four times as much.

One of my side businesses used to be as a project manager on large technical projects. I did this many years ago for a Big Five consulting firm (a term that means nothing to millennials). It was so long ago, in fact, that the tools and terms have changed dramatically. When an opportunity presented itself several years ago to do some side work as a project manager, I grabbed it, but hesitated for quite a while about my "proficiency" in that role and ability to command the same hourly rate my peers were commanding—peers who frequently spouted words like Kanban, Gantt chart, and Agile. I would argue that 97 percent of them had no idea what they were talking about but knew that the term was one of the hip new keywords. There has to be a meme out there of a group of people standing around a water cooler, one saying, "Anyone get that Kanban done?" and another replying, "Working on it. It's agile. I'll get the Gantt chart to you by end of day." They walk away in pairs, one member of the first pair asking, "What's a Kanban?" and a member of the other pair asking, "What's a Gantt chart?" If there isn't a meme like that, there should be. I always thought it would be fun to sit in a meeting and ask people who had the latest IPF report while enjoying responses such as, "Haven't looked at that yet" and "Working on it today actually." I would have given a $100 Starbucks gift card to the person honest enough to ask, "What the flock is an IPF report?" Because, in fact, I'd made it up.

It was my ex-husband who one day reminded me that he's had more than a handful of project managers work for him who have all the certifications available (and commanded an exorbitant salary to go with them) but can't manage themselves out of a paper bag. In the end, I learn fast, and tools only take you so far. The reason I was a good project manager is that I'm a process and change management fanatic (and when I don't own the company, my ability to manage processes seems to increase twenty-fold because there is no emotion or ego tied to any of it). Sometimes, knowing the terms and the tools is only a small step in the right direction. If you don't know how to read people or customize an efficient solution that takes into account personalities and corporate culture, you're hosed.

Earlier in my career as a jewelry designer, I understood my value but not my worth. I knew that my products were of value and were benefiting others. I simply didn't believe that I, as their creator, was worth a strong financial investment. For some reason, I thought that I was of greater value by having products of less worth (monetarily) than I had earned the right for them to be.

As a project manager, I didn't always understand what was being discussed technologically, but I had a phenomenal business partner, Vann Gutierrez, who is a tech genius and still took the time to explain concepts to me with buckets and crayons. In the end, understanding the technology in great detail wasn't my job, but a peripheral understanding helped me have my arms around the project as a whole, which *was* my job.

We often carry that same mentality into our personal lives as well. Often seen as the "smart" ones, the fixers, we're used to getting phone calls from frantic friends or family members, and we're used to wanting to help everyone with everything. Until we learn that we have value and are worthy even without this and that we all need boundaries, this quality will take up all of our free time and some of our time that should not be free time. Either way, it will leave us feeling empty.

When we allow our ego to run the show, we aren't open to what others think or feel. We also aren't vulnerable enough to really make a difference. This is a critical component of my day-to-day work helping entrepreneurs write their books. I say it all the time (and I'm not the inventor of the saying): "Your transparency will lead to someone else's transformation." There is a perception that, as a leader or a CEO or a mom of many, we have to portray that we have it all together all the time. We know a little about everything and a lot about a few critical things. There's nothing we've "never heard of," we never have a bad day, and we have a solution for everything. We never find ourselves rocking in the corner, sucking our thumbs.

That's asinine. Period. And the moment that you position yourself as someone who's never had a bad day or a challenging month or a week of doubt, you lose credibility as well as an ability for anyone currently in that position to identify with you. Your current lifestyle and joy and trips around the globe feel unattainable to others. And if it's unattainable, why bother?

On the other hand, when you're brave enough to admit that you've had your fair share of challenges, people don't decide you're less credible, they decide that you're more credible. Interesting, isn't it? They flock to you. They identify with you. They say, "If she can do it, so can I. She's the same as I am."

Just ask Lewis Howes.

As he revealed in his latest book, *The Mask of Masculinity* (which is a masterpiece; get your hands on it), sometimes when you dare to step out in authenticity, you'll be beyond surprised by the way people respond. People don't follow you because you're perfect. They follow you because you're fallible and vulnerable and strong and resilient as hell. Also, to be clear, no one ever believed you were perfect to begin with.

When you can say, "Bad shit happens, then you get on with living. Here's how..." people listen. Think about it— some of the most influential entrepreneurs have challenging backstories.

Oprah is an obvious example. So are Walt Disney, J.K. Rowling, John Paul DeJoria, John D. Rockefeller, and Andrew Carnegie. I don't know about you, but when I hear any of those names, I picture the "successful" part of their story. What if they never told anyone that they were homeless and on welfare? Or a poor farm boy who liked to draw? Or a constantly hungry factory worker? Or a member of an L.A. street gang who had been in and out of foster homes as a child?

Those are stories of triumph. There were no shortcuts in those stories. No "luck." No trust fund. No hand-out or hand-up. They know what it feels like to be lost. They know what it feels like to "not know." But they also know how to persevere and make the most of their gifts, talents, and interests. They figured out how to value their worth before anyone else. That's what we identify with when the soundtrack begins to play in the background of the movie of their life. That's what gives us hope. That's what makes them real. That's what makes us believe that we can get where they are; because we've been where they were.

This is the type of entrepreneur for whom I will move mountains to work on his or her book. My friend Mike, who I've already mentioned multiple times, is a wildly successful visual branding expert. But, as he reveals in his forthcoming book, he received a knock on his door just a few years ago from a tow truck driver who was there to repossess his car. Eddie Aguilar, with whom I'm also working, speaks about the dire importance of suicide awareness. Years of psychology-based education don't give him the credibility to speak to this; the fact that he sat on his bed with the butt of a gun resting on the floor and his finger on the trigger, combined with the fact that he's personally known as well as spoken with dozens of survivors of suicide attempts as well as relatives of those who sadly ended their lives, however, does.

That said, there is a fine line between being vulnerable and "letting it all hang out." I've watched countless celebrities use their platform to merely "bitch and moan" about something, seeking validation and support from their followers. That isn't exactly the way it's supposed to work. Showing your vulnerable side is one thing; resting on it is another. No one likes to hear someone they've come to admire complain about how "tough" life is. No one wants to feel as though they're going from student to teacher. *That* is what erodes someone's credibility. So be vulnerable. Be open. Be honest. Be humble. Hear people. Let people hear you. And be sure to walk out of that room stronger than when you walked in.

Be the person you show to everyone so that you are that person before any physical evidence proves it. Or don't. Be the person you believe others see you as (if you actually like her). Or don't.

TRUTH BOMB

"There are people less qualified than you, doing the things you want to do, simply because they decided to believe in themselves. Period."

—ALEXI PANOS

Let's talk about feeling self-conscious for a moment, which is a byproduct of not feeling confident about your value and worth. I find it interesting that, much like the word "assume," we naturally perceive the term self-conscious negatively. The definition of self-conscious is "aware of oneself as an individual or of one's own being, actions, or thought." The definition then goes on, however, to include "socially ill at ease." Does anyone else find it "odd" that those two definitions of the same word are side-by-side?

If self-conscious simply means that you're conscious of yourself, why does common theory purport that being self-conscious is a bad thing? That it's a moment of shame or embarrassment? I believe it an incredibly strong quality to be self-conscious. It's a good thing to be self-aware, is it not?

Being self-conscious allows us to be clear about where we really are in our journey, what our strengths are, what our weaknesses are, and the fact that some of our weaknesses are actually strengths.

It's been said that if you change your perception, you change your world. What you pay attention to you'll see more of, whether positive or negative. So start seeing all the incredible good in yourself. Stop the negative self-talk. Do something every single day to increase your belief in your value, and know that, regardless of where you are in the process, you *are* worth.

TIME TO TAKE ACTION

JOURNAL ACTIVITY

- What statements do you make to yourself that you'd never say to your closest friend?
- Can you commit to reminding yourself every day of how powerful you are, how much potential you have, and the fact that you're simply going to continue to move the needle a little bit toward your goal every single day and celebrate your wins?

THIRTEEN

Drama, Be Gone

"I can see that you're upset. Maybe you should post about
it on Facebook in order to help tone down the drama."
—*Unknown*

I
f there is one thing that makes me crazy (and, to be
clear, there are many things that fit that description),
it's unnecessary drama. I'm a no-drama girl. I didn't
used to be this way. I used to love drama, crave it, bathe in
it. But no more. Now it drains me. If I have to have it in my
world, it will have to be in an area that truly matters to
me. Alternately, it has to be in an area that absolutely
does not matter to me. As in, just about any show on
Bravo. I can no longer be in groups where everyone is
bitching and complaining about what's not working and
how much everything sucks. That gets me no closer to my
own goals, and it makes me want to sleep all the time.

Nothing great happens when I sleep (unless I dream I'm touring the world with Adam Levine or on vacation with Omari Hardwick or Sandra Bullock; then it's a totally worthwhile use of my time).

I have an undeniable physical reaction to the energy around me, positive or negative. I've likely been like this all my life without even realizing it. When I was in my high-drama phase, that's what I sought out and attracted, and it felt completely normal. I simply had no idea how negative an effect it was having on my overall life. Now that I'm more aware of that fact, I'm more tuned in to the reasons I feel energized and powerful or anxious and irritated and the ways they likely relate to what's going on around me.

A few weeks ago, I decided to spend a few hours writing at a bookstore downtown. There are only four comfortable chairs (meaning, they are cushioned, not folding) in the community area. Two of them were occupied, and two were available. I snagged one of the available chairs, but the women occupying two of the other three were having a loud, negative conversation about family dynamics. They were lamenting how toxic family members are, the fact that no one ever changes, and how much they weren't looking forward to their respective family holidays this year. It was the very definition of a bitch fest, and within eight minutes, I thought, "I'm not going to make it." I could have switched to a different area of the bookstore, but the damage was already done, so I left.

Every single one of us has occasional drama in our lives. It's unavoidable. As Mark Manson so gorgeously explains in his book, *The Subtle Art of Not Giving a F*ck*, the trick lies in determining which drama you will allow to be a part of your world. Because, my God, drama will come knocking every single goddamn morning, afternoon, and evening, and if you want to let it through the front door it will be more than happy to enter, take off its shoes, and stay awhile.

Make no mistake, some people not only relish in that fact, they count on it. Oblivious as to what to do without drama, it's as much a part of their life as is flossing or telling the kids to please stop screaming (I'm a borderline obsessive flosser).

I find that people are occasionally bent out of shape over the oddest, seemingly most peripheral things. Some woman in Aisle Two clearly doesn't know how to parent her child since said child yelled through the entire shopping trip, and this experience necessitates a two-hour discussion about proper parenting. The family down the street leaves bikes strewn all over their front yard day and night, and this prompts lengthy discussion about why that's wrong. Someone is driving too slowly on the highway, and the approach is to ride their bumper while flashing your headlights at them and swearing. Loudly. For the love of all that is holy, just switch lanes already and be done with it!

Sidenote: I may be sensitive to and defensive of slow drivers because I secretly worry that one day that's going to be Henry. Jack and Henry will both have speeding tickets before they are eighteen. Mark my words. Jack's will be for going too fast. Henry's will be for going too slow. It's fine.

I was recently reading about people who are addicted to being offended, and it suddenly struck me how real of a "thing" that is. It must be a bad habit that's built over time wherein the person has absolutely no idea what to do with herself if she's not actively defending one of her beliefs and wallowing in the misfortune of feeling offended by someone else's.

We see this day-in and day-out on social media, and it's what prompted me to temporarily take Facebook off of my phone. I have a love/hate relationship with Facebook, and it's an area in which I've had to erect a large number of boundaries, many of which I trampled all over before the end of Day One, but I continue trying to find the best approach for me.

I removed Facebook from my phone, but then realized I had to have it on there to do livestreams. So it had to stay. But I buried it in a folder that's almost never opened so that when I do something else on my phone, that big blue and white 'f' isn't staring at me, beckoning me to come inside where all things are perfectly prepped for debate and name-calling.

I used to have a horrible habit of waking up each morning and immediately checking three things on my phone before I got out of bed: my email, my Instagram feed, and my Facebook feed. I've been working for a while now on not even opening my phone until I get the kids dropped off at school. I'd say it works four out of five days of the week and most weekend days, although sometimes I get lax on the weekend. It's almost as though the universe is looking out for me, however, because I'll inevitably open up that feed on a Saturday morning only to be presented with a horrible story about this, that, or the other thing or a post on which no fewer than 87,975 people have commented that the person who posted it is an idiot. It's usually in that moment that I look at the identity of the person who posted it—who is, apparently, one of my "friends"—and ask myself, "Wait...who even is this?"

I have enough drama to manage, and if it's not my circus and my monkeys, I'd like out please. I don't consider the challenging events any of my closest friends are going through as "drama." I consider them unfortunate life events that I'm here to try to help them through while possibly even learning a bit more about myself in the process. So, for me, the moment I realize that what I'm engaged with is "drama" is the moment I acknowledge how unnecessary it is.

Think about it: why does anyone *need* to waste (and it truly is a waste) any of their time on this planet questioning or criticizing the choices or approaches of others, especially when it does not affect him or her in the least? Like, who cares if you chose not to circumcise your son and your aunt or a perfect stranger questions you for it? One, why are you making it public knowledge to begin with? If you're putting your opinion out there, let it be to invite conversation, not to declare the one and only right way to do something. I honestly have yet to see anyone angrily communicate his viewpoint to someone else and have that someone else pause reflectively and then respond, "Gosh, you are so right. Thank you!" (I mean, without an incredible amount of sarcasm.)

People's response to your art or your business is not your circus. It's not your job to own the value others place upon you. It's not your job to defend your position, your prices, or your worth. It *is* your job to own them, which is not always easy, but it is simple.

I once received a scathing Amazon review from a woman who had read my first book, now titled *Holy Sh*t...I'm Having Twins! The Definitive Guide for Remaining Calm When You're Twice as Freaked Out.* Her husband had just been deployed to Iraq, and she said I was insensitive (that was not the exact word she used) because I was complaining about how hard it was to have newborn twins and a two-year-old. The worst part about her review wasn't the review itself—it was so anger-filled that it was clear she simply needed to vent. But the thing is that she wasn't angry with me, she was frustrated by her situation, and it wasn't my job to own that or be apologetic for it.

"You are the average of the five people with whom you spend the most time." When I first heard this, I thought about my close personal circle, and I felt pretty good about it. I am blessed to have found and built lasting friendships with some truly amazing people.

Professionally, however, I was in a "weird" place.

I had a solid five to ten people I looked up to for sure. I watched their live videos, I read their blogs and their emails, I was motivated and inspired by them virtually. But, because those interactions were only virtual, there was a bit of a disconnect. I wanted to be *around* these people, if not daily, at least weekly.

Not long ago, the owner of a Facebook group I'm a member of posted a poll to ascertain what his friends believe makes someone successful. He had four options from which to choose, including a few related to financial success, doing what you love, and having a happy home life. While pondering the options, someone who would become a respected friend—renowned breathing, movement, and meditation coach Chris Tai Melodista— added (and voted for) his own answer (and I'm paraphrasing): "Sensing that they are at home."

I couldn't like or comment on his response quickly enough. That was it. That was when I recognized how to summarize my own definition of *enough*: knowing that I'm home. Not in my city. Not in my house. In my soul.

Defining *enough* in our personal lives is often even more challenging than in our professional lives. You'd think that having to answer only unto ourselves would be easiest, but it's not because it incorporates so many other areas in which we feel vulnerable. Additionally, knowing that we are enough depends upon getting a grip on feeling enough both professionally and personally. It requires looking at an entirely different set of parameters that are emotionally based and extremely personal. When you're running a marathon, the goal is clear: get to the finish line before the streets are re-opened to motorized traffic. When you're trying to become your best self, what's the barometer by which you measure progress?

I set out several years ago with a few personal growth goals to help strengthen the boundaries that keep out unnecessary drama: stop caring what people think if they aren't in my inner circle, learn to respect the power of the pause, be present in every moment, and take better care of my health. At the highest possible level, these are each esoteric goals, so gaining clarity on exactly why each held importance for me was critical to making them a reality.

Caring about what people thought was, quite simply, exhausting and pointless, and it distracted me from my purpose. It was a constantly moving goal post over which I had no control, and it made me feel like I was riding a stationary bike while people threw rocks at me as I wondered why I wasn't getting anywhere.

When I read *You Are A Badass* by Jen Sincero, I had several moments during which I thought, "Ohmigod do I ever have a ways to go before I earn my true badassery accreditation." In my defense, I don't think that someone who already knows she's a badass picks up *You Are A Badass* with the same level of fervor with which I did. It was as though I believed in that moment that, by simply buying the book, the stars would order each other to get into the proper formation required for me to immediately transform into a badass.

People-pleasing is something I have been doing all of my life, and it's something I've had absolutely enough of. Yet, for a long time I wasn't entirely sure how to stop. Here was my (somewhat subconscious) logic: if I help other people, I make them happy. If I've made them happy, I'm valuable. They'll realize how valuable I am and won't want to let me out of their life, and further, they'll want to make *me* as happy as I've made them so they'll up their game and be the best friend/business partner/stray dog they can be.

Reality: I was sucked completely dry by people who took and took and took some more (and, in their defense, why wouldn't they? All the benefits of a great friend with none of the effort? Jackpot.). But the result was, I was completely drained and had nothing left to give to the people who genuinely deserved to be able to count on me when they hit a rough patch.

I feel strongly that People Pleaser needs to be an official diagnosis in DSM-IV or V or whatever Roman numeral the manual has advanced to at this point. We People Pleasers have real, deep-seated behavioral patterns that cause serious disruption to our lives if they aren't thoroughly and consistently addressed. These issues are never fully overcome, per se. They lessen tremendously, but the minute we declare ourselves "recovered," the cycle begins again like clockwork. So we intentionally stay in recovery and are forced to work on it a little less as time goes on, but we work on it nonetheless—especially when life puts us into vulnerable spaces where we believe that making someone else happy will automatically make us happy and that not making them happy will make us bad, miserable people.

One of my greatest challenges is that one of my love languages is Acts of Service. Meaning, that's the way I *show* love. I love to help people. If someone says, "My laundry room is a disaster; I need shelving," I will stop everything and say, "I'm on my way over. We'll go to Lowe's first and foremost. Do you have a drill, or do I need to bring mine?" Never mind the fact that my own laundry room is in a complete state of disrepair or that I have a to-do list a mile long for client work. It doesn't matter because, without even thinking about it, my mind has already decided that if only I go help this person, I'll provide value and then, with any luck, he or she will say, "Cool! This was amazing! Now what can I help you with?" or "This was amazing, *You're* amazing! I'm going to go have it written in the sky so that the whole world knows it and no one ever argues this eternally factual point."

It rarely works that way, however. And the responsibility for that fact does not rest for even a moment with the other person.

Kids who are still having their moms do their laundry when they are eighteen-plus years old are often criticized as "lazy," but let's be real; can you blame them? If you had someone offering to do your laundry every week, wouldn't you take them up on that immediately? Because I would! When someone accepts my offer to redo her laundry room in an afternoon, the exact same psychology is at play.

She's not trying to take advantage of me at all. She's not consciously saying, "I'm going to 'use' Liz, and then send her on her merry way." She's just wired in such a way that she takes my offer literally (which is completely normal and fair, by the way) and takes me up on it. She has no idea (and to be honest, oftentimes neither do I) that I have an expectation of how the whole thing will end (the skywriting and such).

Here's where my challenge comes in: I can acknowledge all of this, but I have a really hard time knowing where to draw the line. If I simply say, "I'm no longer going to offer to help anyone," I'm afraid I'll be seen as...well...unhelpful. I'll be seen as selfish with my time. I'm afraid the person won't think I'm uniquely helpful, and I won't "stand out" from the crowd and be deemed someone super valuable to keep in her life.

My goal is clearly to be seen as valuable. We can agree on that, right? It's one of my "things." I have a need to feel valuable—just for being me. I don't know why I have this need, and believe me, I've tried to trace it back to some life event to no avail. Much like businesses, I've started personal relationships over the course of my life at 100mph thinking I'm in some freaking movie. In reality, relationships grow much more organically than that, and the ones worth investing in are ones that organically grow on both sides. If I think about it for more than a few seconds, it doesn't work for me when someone comes into my life like a bulldozer either! It's simply something I have to be cognizant of while accepting this facet of my personality at the same time.

We have to stop putting so much pressure on ourselves to be everything to everyone but no one to ourselves. We know our role in everyone else's life, but we have no idea who we are unto ourselves. We don't know what makes us happy, what makes us feel whole, what makes us feel valuable beyond being of value to someone else, including our clients!

But the most exciting, challenging, and significant relationship of all is the one you have with yourself. And if you can find someone to love the you that you love, well, that's just fabulous.

—*Carrie Bradshaw, Sex and the City*

There is a fine line between being outwardly arrogant and inwardly knowing your worth. The former is loud; the latter is silent. If you truly know your worth, you don't have to share it out loud. You don't have to constantly defend yourself. Because your worth isn't about anyone but you.

We tend to doubt our worth simply because others don't seem to see it. We work so hard to prove it to everyone and then judge ourselves based on how (or even whether) they respond. Other people's perceptions have, historically, tended to become my assumed reality, which was miles and miles from my actual reality. The disconnect created real inner conflict for me, and giving myself permission to free myself from this was one of the most liberating experiences of my life. Obviously, if someone loses interest in another person because they aren't as famous or connected or wealthy as they'd previously thought, that other person should run. It still stings sometimes, however, to realize that you aren't what someone expected, and as such, are not (even if only in their eyes) "good enough."

There is a huge difference between being alone and being lonely, and it's been said many times that women specifically can be on the floor of Madison Square Garden at a Justin Timberlake concert and feel alone. I'm rarely alone, technically speaking. I have five kids and a dog for heaven's sake. But the number of people who truly know me is very small, and I like it that way. There's a fine line between how much of the "real" you you're willing to put out there for people to see, for fear that if you cross over that line, the magic will dissipate and you won't be shiny anymore.

I'm not alone most of the time, but I feel lonely most of the time. It took me a long time to admit that and be okay with it. It took a while for me to admit that others' perception of me is often not my own reality, and that's just fine. I'm sure that everyone from the adorable soccer mom down the street who's always put together and appears to have the best marriage, most well-behaved kids, most adorable house, and an ever-rotating selection of perfectly fitting yoga pants to Julia Roberts and Jennifer Aniston can agree with this sentiment from time to time. We only see as much of someone as they both allow us to see and are honest with themselves about. I wasn't honest with myself for a long, long time.

Because I was afraid that, in doing so, I would disappoint people.

I've been challenged over the years by the fact that the perception of my life and the reality of it have often been wildly different. I remember eight or nine years ago, I was having coffee with an acquaintance and she asked me to donate to an event at a school in my neighborhood (a school that my kids don't attend). When I politely declined, explaining that I was already contributing to my kids' school, she said, "The PTA isn't going to understand this. They think you're a millionaire." That was news to me (both the fact that they thought it and the notion that I was it!). When the confused look took over my face, she continued with, "You know, you've published multiple books, you have jewelry on celebrities, you fly out in the wee hours of the morning to spend the weekend with other millionaires."

With four published books (now five), a jewelry line that's made its way onto celebrities and TV shows, a regular gig on a local NBC segment, keynote speaking credits, and product launches, several perceptions are alive and kicking. One, I'm extremely comfortable financially. Two, I work my ass off all day every day and rarely sleep. Three, I've got it made in the shade.

All of those perceptions create unnecessary inner and outer drama, so let me clear it all up. One, it wasn't all that long ago that I wasn't sure month-to-month if I'd be able to make the car payment. I'm increasingly aware (as is every entrepreneur and even every "stable" employed person) that such a time could come around again any moment. The knowledge that I live this feast or famine lifestyle often keeps me from enjoying the feast because I'm wondering how long it will be until famine comes back around and I need that overflow of cash to get through the next month.

Partnering up with celebrities or having your product show up on one does not guarantee anything. It can get you a day's worth of heightened sales, yes, but it cannot sustain them. That is *your* job. The next week, that same celebrity will tweet about a new line of lip gloss or new pair of earbuds and buyers will flock to that item the way crows escape *en masse* from a tree or utility wire on their way to their next destination.

Don't spend another second living someone else's perception of your life—especially if it doesn't match your authentic reality. Live your assumption of the person you aspire to be, living the life you aspire to have.

Especially if you're a parent, there are dramatic moments that are sadly unavoidable. I wake up some mornings with a headache and a very strong sense of *I don't want to do crap today*. That feeling quickly transitions to, "Why, Liz, did you ever think you could do this? Sure, Amy Porterfield made it work. David Siteman

Garland made it work. Caitlin Bacher made it work. But you are not them. You are the exception. And not in a good way."

To be clear, I've often felt like this kind of exception. When my doctor says, "Liz, nine times out of ten a cut like this is not gangrenous," I respond with, "Shit. Well *someone* has to be that one out of ten, so you'd better get a surgeon ready." I'm not the one-in-347-million-who-wins-the-lottery kind of exception. I'm the *Holy shit we've never seen anything like this; better bring in the reserves* kind of exception.

One morning, I dropped off the kids, came back home, thought about making coffee, remembered my new bedding, and decided to have a reunion with said bedding. *I'll encourage my bedding*, I thought. *I'll thank it for how happy and content and asleep it makes me*.

And for the next forty-seven minutes, that's what I did. To be a bit responsible to my day, I set an alarm. The minute that alarm went off, I noticed three texts that had come in from my son, Henry, while I was showing gratitude and encouragement to my new, grey, glorious twenty-inch pillows.

>   *8:03am Get me.*
>   *8:33am Mom.*
>   *8:35am HELLO!*

And this is why Do Not Disturb doesn't work well for someone such as myself. I don't think that the judge will accept, "But sir, I have to be on Do Not Disturb so as to complete my work and get a full night's sleep" as an acceptable excuse for leaving my sick son at school a minute longer than necessary.

Or maybe he would. I don't know.

I texted Henry back.

> *Henry, what is going on? These texts sound a bit desperate.*

Crickets.

Mass urgency followed by extreme silence. It's a teenager's calling card and the bane of a mother's existence (one of them anyway).

I figured I'd jump in the shower to get ready for my lunch meeting downtown (and pick up Henry). While in the shower, not hearing back from him, I started to panic.

What if "Get me" was so short because he was passing out? What if he hasn't responded because he's being loaded into the ambulance?

So I jumped out of the shower, thinking I should call the school and inquire as to whether or not an EMT crew had recently arrived on campus. No? Oh good. Why would I want to know that? No reason. Don't mind me.

Just as I wrapped the towel turban-style around my hair, he texted back.

> *Have a bad headache.*

Okay, so he was at least conscious.

> *Do you need me to come and get you?*

Crickets.

Five minutes later, he responded.

> *I'll try to stay. Can you get me later if it gets worse?*

I could. But I also had an 11:30 lunch meeting downtown, a 1:00 phone conference, and a 5:00 meeting with my best friend from high school I hadn't seen in twenty-eight years who just happened to be in town for the first and possibly last time ever. So, I mentioned that yes, I could, and aren't you glad your mother works from home even though she works a lot, and also, I'd have to pick you up before 9:50 when I'm scheduled to depart for downtown.

Sidenote: Where is the government subsidy for moms who truly do have to work from home because, if they didn't, they'd end up in jail for child abandonment?

Anyway, this went on for a while (in between his texts came texts from Grace declaring that she's decided to study abroad her junior year, preferably in Australia even though she took many months to acclimate to being only two hours away). I sat in my office and simply stared at the wall doing everything humanly possible not to park my ass on the couch in front of *Grace & Frankie* with the excuse that they are entrepreneurs so watching the show was, in some odd way, a form of research.

I remembered a section I read in *You Are A Badass* where Jen Sincero suggests that, when a particularly challenging moment hits, we say, "This is good because..." And so, unto myself I said, "This is good because I can write about the reality of this part of being an entrepreneur in a truly authentic, in-the-moment manner. Not the way I remember it feeling 7,860 times, but the way it's truly feeling right now in this moment.

I can write about how important it will be, time and time again, to remind yourself that every single entrepreneur, no matter how successful, has had (and still has) these moments of unplanned drama and chaos. Consider them an annoying test from the universe, a regular life interruption, or a messed-up joke from Satan himself, but know that no one is immune, and the key lies in how (and how quickly) you can train yourself to avoid the unnecessary ones and recover from the rest.

Call someone for a three-minute pep talk. Meditate. Sit there and say I AM [fill in the blank with a positive word] until you believe it. Do jumping jacks. Begin again. BUT FOR THE LOVE OF GOD, DO NOT TURN ON NETFLIX!

TIME TO TAKE ACTION

JOURNAL ACTIVITY

- Where is the drama in your life, personally and professionally?
- Why are you resistant to letting go of it?
- What perceived benefit does it provide (because if it didn't benefit you in some way, you would have let go of it a long time ago)?

FOURTEEN

Comparison Crackdown

"You've played Tetris. You know how it works. When you
fit in, you disappear."
—*Unknown*

At some point around 1998, I wrote a book proposal
for a book to be titled *Dear* with a focus on the
value of handwritten letters. As technology
continued to evolve with incredible fervor, people would,
within a few years' time, begin letting others in on the fact
that they were wildly in love with them via text messages
including indecipherable emojis, a prediction I was having
a rather hard time stomaching. The book would showcase
infamous handwritten letters and feature a large number
of prompts for writing letters to those important in your
life. Agents responded, saying that the art of the
handwritten letter was all but dead. This hurt badly when

letterpress and $9.95 handmade cards hit the scene several years later, and it was one of many lessons I'd learn in the importance of Naysayer Avoidance.

Every single entrepreneur was, at one time, just a regular person with a slightly crazy idea and a whole lot of people questioning his sanity. On the back-end of any successful venture, it's easy to pat the brave soul who came up with the idea on the back and proclaim her brilliant, but only because all of the pieces ultimately came together—likely after an enormous number of hurdles the general public will undoubtedly never hear about. Up until the day any idea is proven "viable," it's just another idea. What would have happened if no one had questioned whether or not you could have a bagless vacuum? Or rubber bands shaped like animals and cars that you wear as bracelets? Or flameless candles? Surely someone (or several someones) told those inventors their ideas were nuts. Surely at some point those inventors questioned their own sanity. But who's laughing now?

If any one thing alone is responsible for entrepreneurs throwing in the towel, it's entirely plausible that that "thing" is comparison. The dangers of comparing ourselves to others on social media have been documented for quite some time. We see the bright spots of people's days, filtered to the *nth* degree. People show us what they want us to see, and we believe that's all there is. We compare ourselves to others without even realizing that we're comparing ourselves to fictional characters!

We look at the Gary Vees of the world and think, "I'm not where he is," but what we fail to remind ourselves of is, "He was once where I *am*." We compare our Facebook ads statistics with someone who has a $5,000-per-day ads budget when we're running on a $5-per-day budget. We assume that the lady at the coffee shop who arrived in a shiny BMW and Juicy Couture sweatpants wearing stiletto heels with her dog on a diamond-encrusted leash is deliriously happy, never considering that she might be hundreds of thousands of dollars in debt (because she is).

I often play Checkers with my ten-year-old daughter, Nina. I never win. I mean, never say never, but I lose nine out of ten games. And I don't let her win, to be clear. Far from it. I'm simply not that nice. Sometimes, she sees a critical error I've made and says, "I could jump all three of those pieces right now, but I won't because I don't want to make you feel bad." My response: "Were it you, I'd jump you in a heartbeat. This isn't an area where I worry about your feelings." At which point, she gives it about two seconds' thought and jumps me. Three times.

Recently wanting a bit of a change, she suggested that we play Parcheesi. We somehow managed to get her thirteen-year-old brother, George, in on the fun. Based on the rules I was given, you have to roll a combination of dice that totals five in order to get a piece out of home base. Nina had two of her four pawns in the winner's circle before I'd gotten even one out of home base. It was absolutely ridiculous. George was living the same boring I-can't-roll-a-five-if-you-pay-me existence I was for the first twelve minutes, but then he managed to get three pawns out, three turns in a row.

By the time I rolled my first five, Nina had two pawns in the winner's circle and the other two more than halfway around the board. George had three out of home base and two halfway around the board. It would have been quite easy and completely understandable for me to have simply said, "I have to go do laundry now" and bailed.

But I didn't.

Every time I rolled my dice, I said, "I'm so grateful for the fives I roll." It didn't work the first eight times, but the ninth time it did. So there. Somehow, on my third turn after that, I managed to roll the exact number necessary to put one of Nina's pawns right back in home base.

And yes, I did.

Long story short, George won the game, but I came in second. Nina, who'd been leading by a landslide since her first turn, came in third. All this to say, never count me (or you) out. The only person in the universe that any of us should ever compare ourselves to is ourselves. As long as we're all working to be better today than we were yesterday, that's the truest and most positive measure of growth to which we can aspire.

When I was first getting started as an entrepreneur, I saw everyone as competition, and my comparison game was *real* strong. Whether someone had a similar product or service didn't even matter. What mattered was: Can I benefit you? Can you benefit me? Are our audience sizes almost exactly the same? Does my name carry weight? Does your name carry weight? It was absurd.

Mostly because, believe it or not, there is room for everyone. All of the competition over numbers and followers is ridiculous because if you partner up, you reach twice the number of people, give your brand credibility, and make more sales. Enough with all the competition. Cooperation is in our DNA. We learn everything we know to live life through cooperation. We're hardwired to be compassionate toward others. We stop when there's an accident or to help someone with a flat tire. Cooperation accomplishes so much: it eliminates loneliness, it incites empathy, it creates a shorter distance to a viable solution, and it allows for genuine connection.

TIME TO TAKE ACTION

JOURNAL ACTIVITY

- Write down 10-20 aspects of your personality that are amazing and that you look for in others!
- Celebrate yourself! What are you *great* at? What do others tell you that you're great at?
- If you were not you, why would you instantly want to be your friend, business partner, or client?

FIFTEEN

I Don't Know What's Going to Happen

"We do not fear the unknown. We fear what we project
onto the unknown."
—*Teal Swan*

When you hate not knowing—which is the second most deeply ingrained, less-desirable quality of mine right after aggressive hypochondriac—the road can be challenging to travel because you simply don't know how many more times you'll have to pivot and when or exactly how your desired goal will be reached. The past is history and the future is fiction. But what I do love about all this "not knowing" is the fact that the past is finished, but the future is moldable.

I remember when the younger of our twins, Henry, was under two years of age and we were battling some developmental challenges. The funny part about all of this (because what is life if we can't find humor in the challenges) is that he was in therapy three to four times per week. By "therapy," I am referring specifically to the physical, occupational, and speech varieties. But still, at sixteen, he will not acknowledge that fact whenever anyone else has a bad day.

"You need therapy," he'll say to some poor, innocent sibling. "I did it. You can do it too."

Um, not really. But whatever.

At any rate, we had literally no idea what was going on with this child. He was delayed in every possible way it seemed, and with a twin brother to compare him to, his delays were magnified, and I became obsessed.

We had fantastic doctors. We tested for everything that could be tested for. At that time, everything pointed to autism, except that he was so sociable and loving, and according to everyone in the medical community, you simply could not be anywhere on the autism spectrum if you had an iota of social skills.

Sidenote: Does anyone remember the story of how he got the nickname The Senator? We were at a family reunion, and a meeting of the local DNC was being held in the lobby of our hotel. Henry, who was terrified of bubble gum and balloons (basically, anything that could pop without warning) marched right through the lobby saying to everyone, "Hi. I'm Henry." I can still see his little face today, and it just makes me want to go take him out for coffee.

I remember all those years ago when doctors continued to run tests and say, "It's not that (thank God), but I just don't know what's going on." I was so strangely happy by the "not knowing" in this instance. Most doctors I've come in contact with need to have an answer. They feel like it's their job, and if they don't have an answer, it means that something is wrong with their intelligence. So they'll give you an answer, even if they aren't more than 1.2 percent sure of it. And so it is that I am forever grateful for the doctors who were humble enough to simply say, "I don't know."

We found amazing therapists, starting with Rian who recommended Gretchen who recommended Tracy (for the record, if any of the three of you are reading this, I will love you forever plus seventeen days) who all said the same thing, "We treat what we see, not a diagnosis."

I remember one particular morning when Henry was about a year and a half old. He was sitting in our family room holding a ball. I walked over to him and said, "Henry, can you hand me the ball?" I put my hand out so that he could give it to me.

He just looked at me.

I repeated my question, and he continued to simply look at me.

But here was the thing: I looked into his eyes and I knew, beyond the shadow of any doubt, that he was in there. I saw the furthest thing from "emptiness" behind his eyes, and in that moment I knew that while we didn't know what we didn't know, we'd sure as shit figure it out.

It turned out that he heavily struggled with auditory processing, which you can't formally test for until a child is around eight years of age. It wasn't that he couldn't hear me (though he'd claim that was the case many times over the coming years) or didn't care. His brain simply wasn't unscrambling my words fast enough to process them.

As I learned, the brain is very moldable at that age. It's growing so quickly, and what we expose it to can make a dramatic difference in how it grows. And that's about all I can intelligently explain about that. Not knowing how it was all going to work out was hard. But knowing that I could find ways to connect the neurons in his brain that weren't properly connected meant that there was hope.

If you met Henry today, you'd have nary a clue that any of this ever went on. He's one of the smartest, kindest, funniest people I've ever known. What this story illustrates is how malleable the brain is and, in tandem, how malleable the future is.

We don't know how things are going to turn out, and for impatient control freaks such as myself, that can be very challenging. But we have the opportunity every single morning to begin again. Enough needing to know the future *just enough* is needing to control everything. In the end, the result is often so much greater (and different) than the one we initially imagined anyway. If we begin every single day with no goal any higher than being a better version of ourselves than we were the day before, how can things not end up okay?

Like, literally, explain to me how that is possible!

This past year, I've incorporated the most profound, life-changing mantra to date into my life (beyond *Enough*, that is).

Are you ready for it?

Okay.

Stop looking like you're still waiting. I just gave it to you.

Okay.

Not "Okaaaaaay?" Just "Okay."

Not a question, a statement.

That's the mantra: okay.

I have spent years of my life trying to figure out the *why* behind other people's choices, behaviors, actions, and thought processes.

Enough.

The mantra "Okay" is similar to "You Cannot Be Serious" or the for-a-bit popular #Wut, but it's far less snarky and far more grammatically correct while accomplishing the same mission.

"Elizabeth, we need you to edit this 120-page contract by morning. Yes, we know it's 6:30pm."

Okay.

"Liz, I think Banks ate your Peppermint Patties. All of them."

Okay.

"Mom, Grace just called me an a-hole."

Okay.

Now, to be clear, the tone behind the word is critical. It's not said with enthusiasm or excitement, but with slightly confused acceptance. Sometimes the 'o' is elongated, sometimes there is a slight questioning lilt at the end, and sometimes it is admittedly said like, "Okay, you cannot be serious. #Wut?" (It's important to audibly include the word "hashtag" before "Wut" for full effect. And, yes, the way you pronounce "Wut" is only subtly but quite clearly different from "what." Just ask any teenager.)

Life is short. I'm an overthinker. These two realities mix like my son George and germs. In other words, not well. Sometimes, many times in fact, the most effective way to move through something is simply to accept it, and saying "Okay" is the most effective way I've come up with for doing that. Which is hilarious because I do not ever express myself with just one word. Ever. Seriously.

As an overthinker, a propensity toward over-analysis also heavily courses through my veins. This is as safe a combination as a house of cards built on a raft floating in a swimming pool on a windy day. When complete nonsense ensues, there are three choices: analyze the living hell out of it (never knowing if your analysis is even close to correct while knowing that said analysis can't change the situation one bit), make it a drama-starter from which commence thirty-six conversations with seventeen different people over the course of five hours complaining about said nonsense, or simply say, "Okay" and move on. Honestly, the latter approach is the quickest way to get from nonsense to normalcy.

Most of us are wired to seek what's next. I'm *clearly* wired that way. Ambitiousness is one thing, but ambition in the absence of ever realizing a goal is just sad, and it has a terribly negative long-term effect. When we're always wondering what comes next, we aren't present with what we're creating. We're on autopilot—which is bad when your autopilot includes unproductive habits.

I once told a friend that I was planning to get a tattoo on my left forearm that read Begin Again. He quickly recommended that, while I was there, I get one on my right forearm that read No Distractions. It's easy to get distracted when we're working toward something we aren't entirely clear about. Some call it feeling blocked. Some call it paralysis by analysis. Some call it a lack of mojo. Some call it sheer exhaustion.

I call it FOWN. It's like FOMO (Fear Of Missing Out) but instead of Fear Of Missing Out, it's Fear Of What's Next, and it's what causes my self-discipline to take a seat in a comfy bean bag on the sidelines. When we don't have a straight line to take us step to step to step, or when the next step in front of us makes us hyperventilate a little bit, it's easy to decide that something else simply has to be done in that moment. Because we're afraid, nee terrified (I've always wanted to use the word "nee" in a book), of what comes next.

Listen, I've tried every possible proposed solution to this problem. I've made to-do lists. I've labeled lists by color. I've tried to group to-dos according to priority (however, what is one to do when twenty-two of them can legitimately be classified as urgent?). I've bought new calendars. I've bought pretty journals. I've bought notepads with funny sayings on them. I've used different electronic calendars. I've set alarms on my phone. I've told my kids not to let me out of my chair until such-and-such was complete. I've switched up my work environment to something with greater energy and to something with zero energy. I've tried breaking my day into segments. I've tried taking cheat days.

I've. Tried. It. All.

In the end, none of it worked until one thing changed—and, not surprisingly, it wasn't my environment or the coffee I was drinking or the bean bag in which I was sitting on the sidelines. It was getting out of my own way, looking the FOWN in the eye, and telling it to sit the hell down and shut the fuck up.

I still don't have a full-fledged, Liz-proof, works-every-day strategy for dealing with FOWN. Therefore, I still fall prey to it occasionally. But I recognize it. And when you recognize something, you can name it. And when you can name it, it becomes real. And when it's real, you can ignore it, but doing so doesn't make it unreal. The whole analogy is very much like the children's book *If You Give A Mouse a Cookie*, come to think of it.

Sometimes, FOWN is expressed by talking too much and wasting too much time celebrating perceived wins that we think we need to communicate to everyone plus 16 strangers.

"You will never believe who just re-tweeted me. Everything is going to take off now. I can totally take the rest of the day off."

"I'm grinding so hard; I haven't slept or eaten or talked to anyone I care about in weeks. That's how committed I am. I can't make my car payment. But I'm damn committed."

"The morning show on our local NBC affiliate just talked about my product for twenty-seven whole seconds. Brace yourselves; we're about the hit the next level. Let's go get coffee while we wait."

Don't get me wrong; those accomplishments and genuine hustle are incredible, and both are absolutely worth being excited about. But they do not, in and of themselves, move the needle. Even if they move the needle for a day (increased traffic and/or increased sales), the onus is on you to stay relevant to new customers. The idea that your business has taken (or will soon take) an uptick and will now stay at that heightened level with no support is unrealistic and sets you up for disappointment and frustration.

In short, note the exciting event and then just shut up already and move on to the next to-do. I have to remind myself of this almost daily, so please don't be offended that I just told you to shut up. It was more of a general "shut up." We announce what we're doing, how hard we're working, and who in Hollywood is talking about it in order to get validation. That's totally normal. But sometimes, it comes down to not needing to announce everything we're doing or every goal we hit.

I recently heard the phrase "Intention doesn't require attention," and it deeply resonated. We claim we're working sixteen-hour days, but we aren't. We take two-hour lunch breaks and drop down in front of Netflix for an hour in the afternoon and sit at our computers while staring out the window or mindlessly scrolling through social media. Most of us are not intentionally, purposefully working sixteen-hour days for more than a few days in a row—at least not productively—because that kind of schedule is simply not sustainable.

This is the exact reason HIIT workouts are so popular (with the masses, not me). It's also why sprints and periods of deep work—which often go together—are so heavily used in business. Most people can benefit their body more with an all-in fifteen-minute HIIT workout three times per week than with a ninety-minute run, six days a week. Same philosophy holds true with work. If you only have an hour a day to commit, make it count. If you only have an hour a week to commit, make sure that hour moves you one step closer to your goal; don't just "work" to say you're working and then feign surprise when the needle doesn't move.

Make sure you aren't so afraid of what comes next that you're self-sabotaging in some way with the result that you are completely, utterly exhausted, but the needle doesn't move.

TIME TO TAKE ACTION

JOURNAL ACTIVITY

- When was the last time you were uncomfortable not knowing how something was going to play out?
- What limiting belief or fear was hiding under that discomfort?
- What can you say to yourself the next time you find yourself worrying about how something will play out in order to remind yourself that everything is happening *for* you, and everything will be okay?

SIXTEEN

Somebody Help Me

"Investing in yourself is the best investment you will ever make. It will not only improve your life, it will improve the lives of all those around you."
—*Robin Sharma*

Early in their careers, many coaches tend to hold tight to an odd belief that, if they are a coach, and they have a coach, they are somehow a fraud. I find this notion extremely confusing and wildly limiting. The very best coaches I know have a coach, all the way up the chain. Tony Robbins has a breathing coach. Enough said.

The most talented hair stylists in the world do not cut their own hair. I know this because I asked my Hair Guru, Jamie, if she'd ever consider cutting her own hair. The look she shot me immediately and irrefutably said, "Hell no." The most talented writers have editors. Many renowned artists greatly admire the work of and learn from other artists. The world's top athletes have trainers. No matter what you're doing, unless you are absolutely the best in the entire world in every single area (and before you suggest that you might be, let me remind you that it's impossible) you can level up. Truly leveling up requires more than just a book or a weekend retreat. Those are part of the program, but they won't create the lasting change that will take you to the next level and keep you there.

I often wonder who Jay Abraham and Melinda Emerson turn to when they need a good kick-in-the-ass or level-up session. Maybe the Dalai Lama, I don't know. But the buck doesn't stop with even the best of the best. Not to mention the fact that it's how they've *become* the best of the best.

Wherever we are in life, we can always go higher. We can always get better. We can always get more focused and more efficient. It's not about finding someone who's better at everything than we are; it's about finding someone who's stronger than we are in the areas we need to focus on. It's critical that you see yourself as your biggest and most secure investment, and if you haven't up until now, start this very minute.

Identify the one, two, or three areas in which you'd like to focus hard on leveling up over the next year. Find someone who can help you do that. Not a friend, not a family member. Someone to whom you truly feel accountable and who won't accept any of your BS excuses. Find someone you wholeheartedly believe is in a place to partner with you to serve your best interests. You're going to have to financially invest, period, in someone who will commit to meeting with you once a week either in person or virtually, direct the course of the train you're riding, and hold you accountable to keeping that train on the track through dark tunnels and precarious switchbacks. Change up the way you think about this investment. Many times, people have a hard time investing in a coach because they aren't completely sure about the return on investment. The irony of that is that if you, too, are a coach, what are your clients expecting to receive as a return on *their* investment? The fact of the matter is, the right coach will ensure that you get more done and grow more authentically in alignment with your goals than you would were you not to work with him or her. Period. That's a phenomenal ROI in and of itself.

It's important to find someone who's ahead of you in the important areas, but not too many steps ahead. Too much difference between where you are and where they are often doesn't work. For one thing, when you choose someone who's years and years ahead of you, the tactics and discipline you require to up your game by just two levels are tactics they haven't had to work on in quite some time. Therefore, coaching you on how to employ them may not be their forte. For another, the higher up the success chain you go the more expensive the coach will be. Hiring a coach who charges $8,000 per month when your business isn't yet generating the revenue to support that can be as stressful as it is unnecessary. If you aren't yet running a six-figure business, you don't need a coach whose skill is getting people from six to seven figures per year. Also, the same coach who will get you to five figures a year likely won't be the right person to get you to six or seven figures a year (or they might). You're looking to surround yourself with a similar energy, a similar learning curve, similar mindsets, and—in group coaching programs—it's helpful when the other participants are in a similar space. High tide raises all boats, remember?

I remember a day—likely more than two decades ago—when I watched an interview with Sir James Dyson (of the Dyson vacuum empire). He said that he had found the greatest success by watching what everyone else was doing...and then doing the exact opposite. Truth be told, I might have fallen a bit in love with him in that moment. There's a subtle difference between reinventing the wheel and disrupting an industry. Doing the former is inefficient. Doing the latter is life-changing.

Think about it. If you have a huge group of people, and when someone shouts "Go!" everyone runs to the East but only one person is brave enough to run to the West, who will you notice? Now, that guy better have something interesting to say once you catch up with him, but as long as he does, he's the one who's going to grab (and keep) your attention. Everyone else in the group may have equally brilliant ideas, but because they are all running in the same direction (sometimes attempting to trample one another in order to ensure their respective victories) they're less noticeable. Except that guy in the neon yellow jacket. But he's looking to stand out for all the wrong reasons.

I used to think it was incredibly sexy to know a little bit about a whole hell of a lot. It was hard—almost impossible—for me to say three little words. No, not *those* three words. I mean, those too, but the three I'm referring to at this juncture are: "I don't know."

I hated both not knowing something and having to admit that I didn't know, whether or not the topic at hand fell within my "area of expertise." Think about that for a moment. If someone asks you a question about an area you don't care about and no one would think you know anything about and you don't know the answer, you likely won't be phased. But, if your area of knowledge is toddler taming strategies while shopping and someone asks you what you think about this new theory called PODA (which I literally just made up), would you be uncomfortable saying, "I haven't heard of that. I'll have to look into it!" or would doing so make you feel like a fraud to the point that you'd subtly reply, "Oh, I think it's kind of...oh hang on, I'm getting an important call" and then put your phone to your ear and talk to...yourself.

Many fit into the latter category. A couple of years ago, I decided that "I don't know" was going to be my mantra that year, and I thrived on it. I saw it as an opportunity to learn. Even in the area of things I did know or had an opinion on, I saw it as an opportunity for discussion, for broadening my own horizons.

When you're running a business, it's critical that you know what your strengths are as well as the areas where you need help. We refer to this as "staying in your lane." Most of us wear all the hats for quite some time out of sheer necessity, but we simply aren't capable of wearing them all well. Beyond what you are and are not proficient at, it's important to be clear about what aspects of your business you actually *enjoy* regardless of whether or not you're good at them. I'm proficient at accounting—but I hate it with a passion.

Know what you're good at, and put your focus there. Acknowledge what you are not good at/don't know much about/hate doing and know that those are the areas you will outsource or ask for help with as soon as possible. There is no glory in pretending to know everything there is to know about every area of your business.

In order to know what you need help with, you have to be humble enough to know what you're not good at. And *none* of us is good at everything. One day, my friend Dara, who is a life coach, asked if she could interview me in an effort to get a better sense of her ideal clients' mindsets and experiences. I wasn't sure whether I should be flattered or offended by the notion that I was one of her ideal clients, and I still haven't been brave enough to ask.

She said, "I wanted to interview you because you are one of the most hard-working people I have ever known."

That is when my eye-rolling began.

"This is when I start to feel like a total fraud," I confided.

She looked at me quizzically.

"I know it seems like I'm working all the time, but would it surprise you to learn that I binge-watched an entire season of *The Real Housewives of Orange County* the other day? I'm always thinking about work, yes. I'm always dreaming the dream, yes. But working? Hard? I don't know."

"Ok," she responded. "Well, you're one of the most driven people I've ever known." Now, that's true. I am driven. When I say I'm going to do something, I do it. But that mostly relates to "I'm going to get a dog" or "I'm going to paint this wall."

When you're building a business, drive on its own is not enough. If you don't pair that drive with an equal or greater amount of focused execution, you're going to be standing in mud most of the time while everyone around you thinks you're a hardworking millionaire and you're wondering how to pay for the shoe cleaning kit for your now-muddy shoes.

There is a reason co-working spaces have grown like crazy. Actually, there are a few reasons. For one thing, there are far more startup ventures than ever before, and most startups have neither the funding for large office spaces nor the furniture and utility bills that come with them (or they have the funding, and they choose to spend it on something with a higher ROI for a few years, like coaching or strategic marketing!). The other reason for the rise in popularity is the degree to which entrepreneurs enjoy working alongside other entrepreneurs. We like the energy, the camaraderie, the understanding of it all. Co-working spaces allow us to network, find like-minded new friends, and feel like we're "at work" (and by this, I mean not be able to turn on the TV mid-afternoon without everyone knowing you're doing it). They provide some of the benefits of being in an office (printer, coffee shop downstairs, mid-afternoon snacks) without having to rent (and staff) an entire office space.

They also allow us not to be alone.

For me, this fact in itself has proven the most valuable reason for utilizing them. Being an entrepreneur is, quite simply, lonely. It's physically lonely much of the time, and it can be emotionally lonely as well. Not everyone will understand (or support) your reasons for going out on your own. As though you aren't worrying enough for everyone on the planet already, people will worry *for* you (and be less than quiet about it) when it comes to providing for yourself and/or your family.

It's hard to stay on track when you're working all by yourself inside the same four walls every day. It can be equally hard when you're in a coffee shop surrounded by strangers who have no idea what you do or where you're trying to go. It's important to acknowledge that the ride to the top can feel awfully desolate at times. It's critical to find other entrepreneurs with a similar outlook (preferably a positive one) with whom to surround yourself.

Leaders need coaches, but they also need incredibly true and trusted friends. We all have a boiling-over point. It's that moment when all of the nonsense from the previous day, week, month, or even year finally spills out of us—and normally, not in a pretty way.

It's usually a seemingly unrelated and wildly unimportant event that pushes us over the edge. That's where they got the phrase "The straw that broke the camel's back" because, of course, it wasn't the straw that did it; it was the straw that added 1.2 ounces too many to the load the camel was asked to carry.

Everyone has a different threshold for boiling over. I remember when Jack and Henry were babies, and I constantly commended my friend Mollie for having such a high batshit-crazy-mode threshold. I swear, that girl could manage bullshit with a smile for years. But then one day, seemingly out of nowhere, the batteries in the clock on the wall that was purely decorative anyway died, and she looked at the clock thinking it was 11:10 only to realize it was actually 2:35. That was the moment when she lost her shit.

I have friends who have experienced events in the past few years that have made their new "normal" nothing short of absurd. And, because they've so slowly acclimated, they don't even realize how stressful life has become or why they are breaking out in hives every third Sunday.

My personal threshold seems to have no rhyme or reason. Sometimes it's weeks. Sometimes it's months. Sometimes it's minutes. What I always find fascinating and hilarious, at least in hindsight, is the event that ultimately pushes me over the edge.

Connection matters. You can Google tips and tricks and strategies all day long (and find them). That's not what people are hungry for. They're hungry for those tips combined with human connection. Someone who "gets" them. You can read post after post of tips and strategies, but if you begin to pay attention, you'll recognize that the people you're paying the most attention *to* are the ones who are working to connect with their audience, not simply preach to them.

TIME TO TAKE ACTION

JOURNAL ACTIVITY

- Talk to yourself as though it's a year in the future. What does *enough* look like in *your* world?
- What would that future you do, say, or feel when the current you is having a tough day?
- If you were your own client, what would you say to yourself? Write this down and read it every single morning and evening until you've assumed it without having to think about it.

SEVENTEEN

I'm Unbalanced

"Some days I drink fresh green juice and work on my abs.
Some days I chase a plate of nachos with a Moscow Mule
and refuse to get out of PJs. It's called balance."
—*Me*

Here's a fact, Jack: Balance is Bullshit.

Ask any person who's ever been in recovery from anything if they're ever "home free." They'll tell you the answer is no (unless they're in denial). It likely doesn't require as much effort to stay in a recovered state as it once did, but it doesn't require zero effort—especially when times get tough.

The same is true with balance. For many years, there was a bit of a revolution on how to find better work-life balance. How to balance kids and work and the garden and grocery shopping and time for self and your hair appointment and keeping the house clean and on and on and on as though there were a magic solution that, once employed, would be the miracle missing spoke that would keep the wheel perfectly spinning.

You know what? Stop. Stop trying to "find balance" as though once you find it, you'll have it automatically and indefinitely. Finding balance is like surfing. You have to adjust. Sometimes more, sometimes less, but all the time. If you get too complacent, you'll just be chilling on your board and a massive wave will come and take you out. Plus, as Fredrik Eklund reminds readers of his bestseller, *The Sell*, "Smooth seas never made a skilled sailor."

I'm just trying to get through the day, people. My days look absolutely ridiculous to most people, but as long as they work for me 95 percent of the time, I'm good. I look at people who go off to a nine-to-five job in a cubicle every day and have no idea how they do it. They look at me and my crazy and have no idea how *I* do it. The key is this: find what works for you and know why. And know what you need to get yourself back into balance when you're out. The answer is different for everybody and every day.

Remember Tommy Baker? He had a great podcast one day about beer, and I've gotten his permission to re-tell the basics of the story here. In a nutshell, Tommy suddenly felt one day like he wanted an ice cold beer. Now, most people would do one of two things in this moment: they'd beat themselves up about the fact that they wanted a beer at noon on a Tuesday, or they'd honor their "inner calling" and go have a beer at noon on a Tuesday!

Tommy took it a step further. He asked himself what the beer really represented. For him, it was, in one word, freedom. He then asked himself, "What am I really craving? And how can I get that beer (freedom) in a way that will get me closer to my overall goals?" (And, to be clear, if he'd decided, "By going and getting a beer!" he would have, and he would not have looked back because that's not something Tommy does.) But he realized that the kind of freedom he was searching for could also be achieved by hiking a nearby mountain. So that's what he did. The beer represented feminine energy, believe it or not, as well as freedom and lightness and letting go and being in flow. A hike would give him just that.

He wondered, "Where can I hike that can give me freedom at a higher dose than one beer?" His intuition told him to go hike Pinnacle Peak (no, my intuition never tells me to do that either, but he's unique). So he did, which put him into nature (which also represents feminine energy). If what he was looking for deep down was freedom, what would serve him better? Having the cold beer or doing a workout at Pinnacle Peak? His intuition told him: go to the mountain. So he did. And he felt highly connected and powerful and in flow.

This made me think; what am I really seeking when I plop myself down on the couch and declare that I need to watch the next eight episodes of *Life in Pieces* or *Power*? I want to feel happy; I want to laugh; I want to stop thinking about my responsibilities; I want to live vicariously through other people.

Sometimes I sit down and watch *Life in Pieces*. Other times, I'll take a walk (which is where I get a lot of inspiration) or read a few chapters of a good book or redecorate my office or work on a room I'm in the midst of remodeling.

Erin recently asked me, "So, how are we supposed to find balance exactly?" My response was, "We aren't." I truly believe that. Balance lives a moment-by-moment existence. Right now, while you're sitting there reading this book, you're balanced, right? You are. Because if you weren't, you wouldn't be sitting down and reading. For the sake of argument, your world is balanced right in this very minute. When it begins to become *un*balanced is when you think about all the things you have to do over the course of the rest of the day, or tomorrow, or this month. Or, when you're in the midst of a task for work and everything is going along swimmingly and then you receive a phone call or an email about something that has to be handled immediately and suddenly your day goes off course. Then you feel "unbalanced." But still, in that moment of feeling unbalanced, you're still balanced in the imbalance. I hope this makes sense because the realization of it greatly helped me. The point is, there is only ever this moment. If it feels crazy, do what you need to do to make it feel less crazy. If it feels great, carry on. Recognize that the fear of or sense of "lack of balance" has more to do with contemplating the details of a future over which you have little-to-no knowledge of or control over in the present moment anyway.

TIME TO TAKE ACTION

JOURNAL ACTIVITY

- When you begin to feel "unbalanced," what is going on around you?
- What is it that you feel you don't have control over?
- How can you take back the power to own those moments?

EIGHTEEN

It Won't Work Because...

"The only thing keeping you from getting what you want is the story you keep telling yourself about why you can't have it."
—*Tony Robbins*

"You're doing *what*?"

"I don't know if that's going to work."

"Really?"

"Hmmm."

And my favorite response of all after you tell someone any new idea related to your business: complete silence.

These are the responses we often receive from others when we tell them about our big ideas, our dreams, our plans for the future. Many times, these responses come from those closest to us, which makes them even more difficult to stomach.

Those can all be hard words to hear.

You know what are harder words to hear?

The ones we say to ourselves when we think about our big ideas, our dreams, our plans for the future.

"Can I do this?"

"What if I fail?"

"What if everyone thinks I'm irresponsible or stupid?"

"How will I get the word out?"

"What if no one likes it?"

"What if no one will pay me what I'm charging?"

"What if the client who just signed on to pay me what I'm charging was the last one who will ever agree to my prices?"

"What if I can't pay my bills?"

"What if I prove my parents right?"

"Who am I to think I can pull this off?"

"What if I make people sad?"

The list goes on and on.

We often think that Step One is quieting others' voices and Step Two is quieting our own voices. But what we often fail to realize is that in order to do the former, we must first do the latter. As much as I wish we could take our heads off our shoulders sometimes, to date I haven't been able to figure out how to make that work. So until Google or some AI guru perfects it, I'm stuck with my head on my shoulders and my brain in my head.

Therefore, the words I most need to quiet are my own. In fact, rather than quiet them, I need to change them.

We each have to learn to be our own best advocate and motivator. If we don't believe in ourselves, how can we expect anyone else to believe in us? If we can't, of our own free will, return to our inner power and constant opportunity to begin again each time it's required, who do we think is going to more strongly encourage us to do so?

If someone has a great new book or product or service, and when you ask her why others should invest in it, her response is a sullen, "I don't know. I think it's kind of cool and it'll probably make you happier," would you be interested in their product?

I didn't think so.

You have to believe in you more than anyone else does. It has nothing to do with arrogance or believing you're better than anyone else. It's about knowing and believing in your unique value and gifts.

I've always been an extroverted introvert. That's a thing, right? I think the technical term is ambivert but that makes me think of frogs or salamanders, which I know are amphibians, not ambiverts, but maybe some of them are both. I don't know. Basically, it is my custom to stand on the periphery of almost every situation, simply surveying it. Once I'm more comfortable, most people wish I'd go back to being uncomfortable because, once relaxed, I never shut up.

Many years ago, the idea of approaching anyone I held in even remotely high esteem was unfathomable. My limiting belief was: why would a celebrity or other important person take time out of his or her day to talk to me? I have nothing to offer them in return.

Julia Roberts changed all that. Yes, Pretty Woman Julia Roberts.

When her twins were born, I thought, "Oh, what can it hurt?" and sent a copy of my first book to her in care of her agent or manager or somebody I was 39.6 percent certain was affiliated with her in some way. I did what, at the time, it was said you should do: use a brightly colored manila envelope and make your presentation attractive so it would stand out in the eyes of whomever had the job of getting it from the post box to the celebrity.

I literally sent it off thinking, "I hope it makes it." That was the goal—just to get to her. I didn't have a thought in the least that I'd ever hear a word from her people and certainly not from her directly. One day, I went out to get the mail, and there was a pale yellow envelope hand-addressed to me with no return address. The postmark noted Santa Monica, CA, but other than that, there was no indication of the sender.

This was before the days of Anthrax scares, so I opened it.

It was a thank you note for the book. It was at least five sentences long. And it was signed, "Love, Julia."

You Cannot Be Serious, I thought. Surely this is from her assistant, which is still really nice. I mean, the woman must get a lot of mail! But the longer I looked at it, I thought, "This is clearly written by a left-handed person." I know this because my sister is left-handed and she writes certain letters in similar ways. So I Googled, "Is Julia Roberts left-handed?"

Answer: Yes.

Will I ever know 100 percent whether Julia herself wrote that card? No. I mean, not unless she'd like to meet me for lunch someday and confirm it with a wink, but I'm relatively sure that she did. It seems like something she would do.

I thought, "If Julia Roberts can take the time either to write a substantial thank you note to someone she doesn't even know or hire an assistant and direct him or her to write thank you notes, there is not a single celebrity on the planet who can use their celebrity status as an excuse for being "too big" or "too busy" to communicate with someone else on a human level.

The bottom line: I sent her a gift, and in her world, one says Thank You for that. So she did. The End.

But it opened my eyes to how approachable people really are, and certainly today with the onset of social media, they're more approachable (and, simultaneously, more often approached) than ever before. The idea that you can't reach someone for an interview, an endorsement, or an opinion is absurd. Will everyone respond? No. But is there any reason at all not to try? No.

One of the things people don't know about me is that nearly all of the big PR hits I've had have happened without a hired publicist. They've happened because a genuine connection I made "coincidentally" panned out. If you make genuine connections, good things happen.

I have a beautiful friend in LA named Gregory Zarian. He is an angel on Earth, I swear, and one of my favorite people.

And we've never met in person.

I was supposed to do a segment years ago on *The Rachael Ray Show* with Gregory's identical twin brother, Lawrence (who is known as The Fashion Guy). It was going to be a makeover of a grown set of multiples. Somehow the producer heard about my first and second books and emailed me to see if I knew of any adult identical triplets or quadruplets. Who knows how, but I just happened to have heard about a set of identical triplets, two of whom were living in the United States and one was living overseas. She wasn't sure how she'd get a hold of them, but she somehow did, and they were scheduled to come on the show. She reconnected with me and said, "I'd love to have you come do a segment one day with Rachael for moms of newborn twins." Of course, I would have loved to do that, but that producer left the show shortly thereafter and took my dreams of sitting on set with Rachael with her.

But somehow—and the somehow is completely lost on both Gregory and me at this point—I ended up connecting with Gregory instead. I think I made him some jewelry and then he started recommending my jewelry and his friends began asking for it. Anytime he wanted a custom wedding gift, he called me. Here was a guy who was all over Instagram playing with the kings and queens of daytime TV, modeling all over the world, and able to connect with any jewelry designer he wanted. But he called me. And I'll never stop being grateful. We talked about doing a line together, and once I had a dream that he wanted me to make a commercial in an afternoon with green screen backgrounds advertising kids' toys (it was a nightmare), but the point is: he's approachable.

The scenario wherein one of my cuffs was worn on *The Today Show* for the full four hours by Kathie Lee Gifford arrived through similar circumstances. Erin was invited to a launch party for a new cooking channel being hosted at the resort of nearly everyone's dreams in Paradise Valley called, appropriately enough, Sanctuary. She was allowed to bring someone, and she asked me to go along. Sure! I mean, I'd stand on the periphery until I got comfortable and then I'd jump in and possibly ruin her entire reputation with my very loud laugh but yes, I'd definitely like to go.

The stars of one of the channel's shows, The Casserole Queens (Crystal Cook and Sandy Pollock), were there and they were absolutely beyond kind. The fact that they were decked out in 1950s attire and chunky pearl necklaces with their hair curled up at the ends did not hurt their already approachable presence. Before long, the four of us were like old friends. Erin had suggested that I take some leather wrap bracelets with the show's tagline on them, which I (extremely hesitantly) did. I kept them in Erin's purse until a time when it seemed authentic to pull them out, and I knew that if that time didn't present itself or the energy was off, in her purse they would stay.

Obviously, they didn't stay in her purse because I loved these girls.

Fast-forward a few months, and The Casserole Queens were scheduled to appear on *The Today Show* to promote their latest cookbook. Crystal called me and said, "Why don't you make some bracelets for the producer and the show's hosts?" I literally thought I was being punked. Who does that? Who gets invited to be on *The Today Show* and then thinks of this tiny jewelry designer they met for an hour at a launch event months prior?

Crystal and Sandy do. That's who.

So I began creating one-of-a-kind creations (using vintage kitchen tools and silverware) for everyone and their brother (almost literally; I was terrified of leaving someone out) as well as additional pieces for Crystal and Sandy as a *Thank you so much ohmigod how do you even say Thank You for this sort of thing* token of my undying appreciation. I packaged them all up such that Martha Stewart herself would have approved, and I sent them off.

And then the segment was canceled.

As often happens, a major, world-impacting news event usurped their segment. *Oh well*, I thought. I was truly far more disappointed for them!

And then Crystal emailed me: "We're going to send off your package anyway."

Uh, what?

Yep. They were sending a big shipment of books to the show's producers, and they put my jewelry in the box with them. I seriously did not think that there was more than a sliver of a chance that they'd ever reach their intended recipients. And then, a few weeks later, as I sat in the earlier-described co-working office space I'd invested in, I was notified that I'd been mentioned in a tweet.

Now, this happens somewhat often. Not because I'm important or known but because I'm frequently mistaken for Elizabeth Lyons, the rising country singer. I won't lie—seeing a tweet that says "@ElizabethLyons rocked it out last night" is, for half a second, extremely awesome.

But this particular tweet actually tagged me correctly, and it was from Katie Lee Gifford's account with a photo of her showing off the custom cuff bracelet I'd made her.

Well.

Thankfully for them, the majority of my office was out to lunch (literally). I skipped down the hallway while squealing. I was truly beyond. And, to be clear, it wasn't about who had worn the cuff or thinking it was going to launch my career (I knew better than that by then). It was because of how thrilled I was that my notion that simply being authentic and building real relationships and genuinely supporting other people nets the most effective PR you can have. And it's free!

People are just that—people. I think they enjoy hanging out with people who are "like them" because they don't have to question their intentions in wanting to be their friend, but one's ability to reach out to someone—be it a local celebrity or an international one—exists.

I've forever been curious about people who've written me emails, and when I write them back, they say, "I never expected you to respond!" Um, why would I not respond? You took the time to write me, so I'll take the time to respond! (Unless you took the time to write me just to tell me you don't like me. I don't respond to those, but thankfully I've not yet gotten very many of them).

I remember when I first approached Jim Steg, a local custom builder, after he was tagged in a social media post with Tommy Baker. His name sounded familiar, and I may or may not have been channeling my inner desire to flip a home in downtown Phoenix. Truth be told, that wasn't what compelled me to contact him; it was what compelled me to friend-request him. What compelled me to contact him was his incredible perspective on his line of work—I remember him replying to one of my Facebook comments with, "I'm not building homes; I'm building relationships." And you could see that playing out daily through his consistent, uplifting posts.

As I would come to learn, Jim is one of those people who has been through the challenges and come out the other side so grateful and whole because of them. He's done the work. (In fact, that's at least one of his corporate and personal mottos: Do The Work). I used to look at Tommy and Jason Sani and Tommy's fiancé, Taylor, and think, "Well of course they're doing this; they're young and not yet managing kids, carpools, and more laundry than is reasonable." But Jim is older than I am (which means he's older than 36, an age at which I managed to freeze myself a certain number of years ago), and he's still on Camelback mountain every morning at 4:30 and posting photos of date night with his clearly beloved wife at least three nights a week.

So I asked him to meet, and to be honest, I didn't have a purpose for the meeting, a fact I casually mentioned as we sat down at his kitchen table. I think I literally said, "I'm not even 100 percent sure what my goal is here." Because I wasn't. I just knew I wanted to be in his space and see where it went from there. I've already learned so much from Jim, all because I was comfortable enough to reach out and ask, "Can I take you to lunch?"

Not everyone has time for that. Not everyone will make time for that. Some people want you to *think* they don't have time for that while they're sitting at home staring at the fish tank. (They might want to read the chapter on being self-aware). Everyone starts out as "no one." Every famous person was, at one time, not known by anyone outside their personal circle. And many of them are humble enough to remember that as well as intuitive enough to sense when they just have a feeling about someone and decide to take a meeting with them even though it perhaps makes no logical sense.

So the bottom line is, approach people! Reach out! Be authentically you. Don't lead with, "I was wondering if you'd endorse this for me." Get to know what drives someone. What are they passionate about? What did they post that you identified with (and why)? How can you provide value to them? *Build real relationships!*

I have yet to meet Gregory Zarian face-to-face, and I am 100 percent confident that if I were in a bad situation, I could call him and he'd help. I hope he feels the same way about me because I'd be on the first plane to LA were I ever to get that call, no questions asked. Same with Jenna McCarthy, for the record, who is likely reading this right now and saying aloud, "Um, Hello? We have that exact kind of relationship. Where am I mentioned in here?"

Right here, my darling, spirited, talented friend.

I won't bore you by going into massive amounts of detail about the inner-workings of my and Jenna's friendship (which has gone on for over eight years now and we've yet to meet face-to-face as well—though I did recently read that Elizabeth Gilbert and Cheryl Strayed have been friends for many years and only recently met in person for the first time. So, Jenna, we're like that, and when we do get together it's going to be ridiculous, and I apologize in advance to everyone who's within 1.3 miles when it happens).

"I'm not [fill in the blank] enough to contact so-and-so" was but one of my limiting beliefs. I've unearthed many others, many of which shocked the heck out of me because they are beliefs I genuinely counsel my own clients out of with frequency. Work to identify your limiting beliefs—all of them. Then, figure out what's underneath them. That's where the solution lies. One of the limiting beliefs that stuck with me when I was designing jewelry was, "I don't have the right to charge high prices for my jewelry since I'm not formally trained as a jewelry artist." The statement that disproved that was, "Complete strangers have happily paid me high-dollar amounts for pieces and then written to tell me how much they love and will cherish the final product." So my new belief became, "I used to think that I couldn't charge what my pieces were worth because I'm not formally trained. But my customers value my work and are glad to pay me more than feels comfortable for it."

TIME TO TAKE ACTION

JOURNAL ACTIVITY

- Make three columns on a piece of paper.
- Write down the left side of the page your limiting beliefs without giving them too much thought.
- Now in the middle column, write down something that disproves that limiting belief. For example, if your limiting belief is, "I can't eat spinach," you might write in the middle column, "I ate spinach last week inside lasagna."
- Then, in the far-right column, write your new belief: "I don't like spinach by itself, but if it's sandwiched between noodles and cheese, I'm good to go."

NINETEEN

Just Do What They're Doing

"Those who follow the crowd usually get lost in it."
—*Rick Warren*

One day I read that Dunkin' Donuts was thinking of changing its name by dropping the "Donuts" portion. I was so perplexed I almost had to drive through Dunkin' Donuts for 40 Munchkins—that is, if they were still selling them.

Dunkin' Donuts has been Dunkin' Donuts for as long as I can remember. When I was little, there was one right behind our church, and every three months or so we'd get to stop in after a particularly riveting Sunday School session and get a dozen donuts. There were four people in my family, so I'll let you do the math. My mom positively never ate three donuts, so my sister and I may or may not have eaten more than three in a day. It's fine. Every time I walk into a Dunkin' Donuts, the smell takes me right back (not that I walk in that often).

The story on their apparently impending name change was that they are trying mightily hard to compete with Starbucks. Now, what is Starbucks known for? Coffee with some food options on the side. What is Dunkin' Donuts known for? Oh yes, donuts. With coffee on the side. If you want coffee, you go to Starbucks. If you want donuts, you go to Dunkin' Donuts. It's quite simple.

In an effort to become known as a beverage-centered brand, they thought to drop the word "Donuts." Now, what I can tell you is that I'm not going to a place called Dunkin' anytime soon, if ever. What's interesting is that they want to be known for one thing, but they have an established brand identity as another. They aren't going to capture Starbucks' market because people are loyal to Starbucks. It's like Target versus Walmart. Or Sam's versus Costco. Or Staples versus Office Max.

When you get to the point where your business strategy is to follow not what *your* customers want but what you perceive to be the most common overall want, you're heading down a bad path. Your customers are going to defect, and new customer acquisition is neither inexpensive nor as easy as simply saying, "We're the new Starbucks." There's a lot more that goes into a brand than product availability. I've never worked inside a Dunkin' Donuts, but I work in Starbucks all the time. I'm unclear how the executives think that simply removing a word from the name they've had for nearly seventy years is going to alter the overall brand identity in the minds of both current and prospective customers.

We spend a lot of time following the leaders (or, as the practice is often referred to: keeping up with the Joneses). We think, "If I can just do what he's doing, I'll have it made." But none of us can do *exactly* what someone else is doing because we are not that person! What we need to do is use our own unique skill sets, personality quirks, and life approaches and let those shine through. That is the quality that can't be replicated. That's the "secret sauce," as they say. A product, a service, a donut—those can all be replicated. But the feeling someone gets when they come into your store or follow your program or read your emails is what keeps them around. If you're switching it up all the time to "be like so-and-so," your customers see that, and they may not know why, but they get confused, and it becomes very easy for someone else to grab (and hold) their attention.

I'm a bit sarcastic. I embed stories and a few swear words into my videos and my writing. If I tried to be just like someone more serious, it wouldn't work because it wouldn't be genuine, and people would see that. If I tried to be over-the-top like, say, Chelsea Handler or Amy Schumer, it also wouldn't work. Mostly because I get really uncomfortable saying p*ssy in public. I'm getting better at it, but still have a ways to go before I have Chelsea's or Amy's comfort level in that area. My customers aren't

290 • ELIZABETH LYONS

their customers—or they are, but they're clear about the reasons why they follow both of us. It's similar in concept to the way we all have different friends for different reasons. I have four best friends, and while they get along with each other just fine, they aren't each other's best friends. They are alike in many ways, which is why they are all my friends, but I get different things from each of them. The same goes for my mentors.

If I want inspiration, I go to Marie Forleo or Jay Shetty.

If I want motivation, I go to Gary Vee or Russ Ruffino.

If I want brutal honesty, I go to Julian Rosen or my mother.

If I want to crack up and be reminded that very little needs to be taken super seriously, I go to Aziz Ansari or Anjelah Johnson.

If they all served the same purpose in the same way, I wouldn't have a need for all of them. It's precisely because they are their own unique selves, providing wisdom and hope and inspiration and honesty through their own particular approaches that I value each and every one of them!

I've combined the words of two of my favorite mentors, Marie Forleo and Jen Sincero, to form one statement that I live by every single day:

"Everything is figure-out-able once you make the
decision that you are un-fuck-with-able."

You are more than welcome to claim it for yourself as
well.

TIME TO TAKE ACTION

JOURNAL ACTIVITY

- Who is your go-to person when you need
  inspiration?
- Who is your go-to person when you need
  motivation?
- Who is your go-to person when you need brutal
  honesty?
- Who is your go-to person when you want to laugh
  until it hurts?
- Who is your go-to person when you need to
  remember that everything is going to be okay?

TWENTY

But When? And Exactly How?

Flow with everything; force nothing.
—*Me (again)*

'Ve saved the most delightful tidbit for last because I love the kind of feel-good drama that I can control. There is a step in this mess that not many are talking about. You have the *what*, the *why,* and the *how*. But there is a fourth and equally critical step: *You have to forget about the intricate details of the how*. You must have openness. Faith. Trust. You must surrender to that which will occur to satisfy your *what* and your *why*.

"Oh, what a coincidence!"

It's become such a cliché phrase, and even I'm guilty of using it on occasion, but I quickly catch myself because I don't believe in it. At all. There is no such thing as coincidence. And if you believe that the universe won't put exactly who you are meant to meet in front of you at precisely the right time, I offer you this as proof that you're...well...wrong.

I remember the first two times I became physically acquainted with the concept of energy. Both occurred in Sedona, Arizona, which happens to be one of the energy capitals of the world. I'd read *The Secret*, I'd made vision boards, I'd heard all about people who simply visualized the dream and then opened the garage door and there it sat wearing a tiara and gold-plated boots, but I'd never truly experienced it up close and personal.

On both occasions, I was at a spa called Mii Amo, which for the record, I can't recommend highly enough. I tell everyone, it's only expensive the first time because, after that, the benefits to your spirit are so magnanimous that you simply ignore the financial cost—you view it 100 percent as an investment in *you*—and this is coming from someone who had Visa pay for both trips.

The first experience was perhaps fifteen years ago. It was my first trip to a spa like this, period, and I had little idea what to expect. I understood as best I could that there were vortexes (is the correct plural form vortices?)

all around the resort, and people experience incredible moments of introspection and clarity while there, but as usual, I was trying too hard and felt absolutely nothing.

I was there with my mom. We were taking a hike and looking for a vortex, any vortex. We kept coming upon barrels made of wire that held rocks, and each time we were certain that we were standing in front of a vortex. So there we stood, silently, reverently worshipping the vortex, waiting for lightning or the idea of the century to strike. When nothing happened, we decided we were overthinking it, so we moved on to the next vortex.

Turned out, those "vortexes" were just trail markers. I want you to please take a moment to imagine all the people walking by, observing us with our heads bowed and hands in prayer, worshipping a trail marker. This is my life, people.

One afternoon during that trip, I had a Reiki session. I lay face-down on the table and my session began. Within a few minutes, I was becoming confused as to why the therapist was rhythmically pushing on my calves. It felt lovely, but this was supposed to be an energy session, not a massage, and the control freak in me became confused that I was in the wrong appointment and some poor soul was sitting in the waiting room wondering why her masseuse had forgotten her.

"Quick question," I said in a whisper. "I thought Reiki involved balancing energy but not with physical touch?"

"That's correct," the therapist replied.

"So how come you're pushing on my calves?" I asked.

"Elizabeth, I want you to very slowly turn your gaze to your calves," she instructed with the calmness of an angel. What happened next blew my mind.

I did as instructed and noticed that her hands were floating approximately three inches *above* my calves. And I could still feel the rhythmic pressure of my calves being "kneaded" and the warm, tingly sensation created from being massaged.

"You have very strong energy in and around your legs," she explained. "I haven't physically touched you once during this session."

Approximately eight years later, I returned to Mii Amo (it took me eight full years to recover from that Reiki session). I met a lovely couple in the common area just after checking in. Probably in their mid 50s, they were a little bit "out there" according to my initial assessment. They were extremely kind and almost uncomfortably peaceful, and I had to wonder if this was their demeanor every minute of every day. Did they ever just bust out laughing for absolutely no reason whatsoever? I could not envision that.

A group of eight to ten of us attended an aura reading session later that afternoon. The point of this session was to learn how to see someone's aura. Let's just cut to the chase. I was the only one in the room who couldn't see (or, at least, was bold enough to admit that she couldn't see) anyone's aura. I relaxed my mind. I squinted. I was like Rachel in the *Friends* episode wherein she first sees her baby on ultrasound and says, "Oh, there it is! I see it!" and then Ross asks, "Do you really?" and she admits, in tears, "No!"

Everyone around me was giddy with their newfound ability to see everyone else's aura, sometimes even two or three layers deep, and I was the inept loser in the room who could see absolutely nothing.

"You're trying too hard," the guide said.

Um, ya think? Clearly he did not read my intake questionnaire wherein I'd listed "chronic overthinker" as one of the three main reasons I was there to begin with.

When he read my aura, he said it was only one color: light blue. He opened his reference book on what each of the colors tends to mean in terms of someone's profession and said, "Light blue is associated with only one profession."

It's going to be a fucking rocket scientist or something else that makes zero sense, I thought.

"A writer," he said, abruptly turning away to answer someone else's question.

Whether or not that's true, and whether or not he'd studied my profile before coming into the session, I don't know (I have a skeptical side; have I mentioned that?), but I did spend some time that evening wondering why he'd pay attention to my profile in one area but clearly not in others before finally considering the idea that, perhaps, just maybe, *writer* was in my spirit all along regardless of whether I studied it or nurtured it or honored it or cared about it at all.

After the aura-reading session ended, our group stood together on the front steps of the spa. The couple I referenced earlier (who could, of course, instantly read *everyone's* aura including those of a few people I'm pretty sure weren't even visibly in the room), stood with us. I can't remember their names to save myself, so I'll call them Peter and Marilyn. A woman from our group was standing on a step with a large tree behind her. The entire area was serenely and beautifully lit by lanterns hanging from tree branches.

Peter said to her, with an almost chilling degree of calmness, "Someone is standing behind you." She turned around, but no one was there.

"Spiritually, someone is standing behind you," Peter clarified.

By this point, we'd all been experiencing or at least hearing about spiritual "stuff" for two days, so while perhaps slightly confusing, the notion that a spirit was standing behind someone had lost its ability to panic any of us.

Peter went on to describe the person he was seeing, and the woman said, after catching her breath, "That's my sister. She died a few years ago."

Peter asked what she died from.

"We don't completely know," the woman said. "The official reason was a heart attack, but they couldn't identify the exact cause of it. It seems to be something genetic, but no one can figure it out, and it's scaring everyone because no one knows what to look for or how to take any kind of precautions."

"She's showing me the letter C," Peter said. "It's a vitamin or a mineral of some sort. A deficiency."

"Yes, that's what we were told," the woman affirmed, becoming more animated and engaged in the experience.

"Cadmium," Peter revealed. "It's a Cadmium deficiency. When you get home, check with your doctor. Just have him check your Cadmium levels."

At this point, I'd had enough. Seriously. I was kind of pissed, to be honest. I felt like, "Who is this guy? This poor woman has had this horrible tragedy and he's acting like her sister is standing behind her telling her how to take care of her health. This has to be so painful for her!"

I've never been one to outright say to someone, "Who the hell do you think you are, playing with this person's emotions this way?" but I suppose I semi-suggested it by saying something along the lines of, "Ok, I'm equal parts fascinated and skeptical right now." I went on to explain my challenges trusting this "energy stuff" that I couldn't see, from my Reiki experience years earlier to the aura reading session we'd all just participated in.

"Do you want to feel energy?" Peter asked me.

Yes. Yes I did.

He started doing some things with his hands. It looked a bit like Tai Chi (I mean, from what I've seen of Tai Chi anyway), kind of forming an imaginary ball of air. After a few minutes, he held that imaginary ball—about twelve inches wide—in front of me.

"Put your hand in front of this ball, flat, as though you're going to touch it with your fingertips first," he instructed. "Now close your eyes."

I did that.

"Now, slowly move your hand forward. Don't open your eyes. Just move your hand forward toward where you know my hands are and see what you feel."

I swear on all that is holy in this entire world that after moving my hand forward three or four inches, I felt warm, dense resistance. I could have pushed through it if I wanted to, but it was an absolute, undeniable change in the density of the air. I slowly pulled my hand back and did it again. And again. And again. I played with it, fascinated, with the biggest smile on my face.

"You're feeling that, aren't you?" Peter asked.

I opened my eyes and all I could do was smile. And then everyone else wanted a turn so Peter's attention turned to them and they were all, "Let me feel it! Let me feel it!" while I just stood there smiling.

To this day, I have no idea what came of the Cadmium revelation. I don't know if that sweet woman was able to identify a missing piece in her family's medical history and put a stop to the unexplained heart condition. I certainly hope so.

But that was the moment, under the trees and the lanterns and the millions of stars when my feeling about forces that we cannot see became more than simply a wondering. It became a belief, and I never could have known in that moment that, while it would take years and years for me to incorporate that belief as a part of my daily life (taking the place of a bit of the forceful-thought-created reality I'd engaged in since forever), it was as though my face wasn't what was smiling. My spirit was. Because I was finally aware of this friend who's always been there, even though you can't see her with your eyes.

I have heard time and again that, while you have to have a plan (and you do), and you have to fiercely execute your plan (and you do), there are some aspects of the *how* that are simply out of your control. You have to trust that the universe will move things around in whatever way is necessary to get you what you want once you're truly ready.

I did believe all that to a degree. But I had a hard time rationalizing the difference between working intentionally and the *how* simply manifesting out of the Southwest when you were so sure it lived in the Northeast. That said, there was a point in my journey (probably that Saturday in Lululemon) when I definitely became open to anything that *wasn't* the way I'd been doing it all along.

A "weird" occurrence happened in my life early in 2016. I had somehow, some way, become Facebook friends with someone who happens to live nearby (all surprisingly-happily-married as well as now-in-jail stories begin this way, do they not?). He's significantly younger than I am. He's got so much energy, drive, and vision that it at once impressed, confused, and terrified me. I wondered, "How did he know so early on in life what he wanted to do? And how did he get such bold confidence?" So I started following his posts.

Because Facebook is so smart, it began recommending that I become friends with his friends. And so, when someone seemed interesting, I did. The infamous Six Degrees of Kevin Bacon kicked in and Facebook began recommending that I become friends with someone with whom I had twenty mutual friends (which was extremely odd given that I hadn't met nineteen of them face-to-face).

A young nutritionist named Jason Sani struck me from the get-go, though I couldn't put my finger on exactly why until I met with him in person. We met to chat about his forthcoming book, *Making Healthy Taste Good* (it's now out, and it's fantastic). For starters, he brought me something that was reported to be both chocolate and incredibly healthy, and I'm sorry that I ate the entire tub of it while we were chatting because, did I mention, it was both chocolate and healthy? They say everything in moderation, but I swear I was more toned when I left that meeting. Jason simply has an energy about him that *feels* good. Sitting across from him, having never before met him, chatting about his book and his challenges and his incredible drive at his age put a smile on my face just like the one I got after sticking my hand into Peter's energy ball (that sounded weird).

What I've found is that, many times, great mentors run in packs. They don't do so on purpose—it doesn't start that way—but it ends that way because their energy brings them together, and then they can't remember a time when they didn't know one another. When you look at Marie Forleo's current group, it includes Glennon Melton, Brené Brown, Kris Carr (and Oprah). They all have retained their sense of human-ness and vulnerability, but they do not think small. They don't live small. They protect their own boundaries (and Brené probably provides the counseling necessary when they slip in this area!). I admire them. I look up to them even if they're younger. I enjoy learning from them. I love their energy and I absorb it and allow it to help fill me up.

There is another Facebook group I spend little-to-no time in because it's huge. I mean, the number of members is nearing six figures. There's a lot of great conversation, in fact I'd argue that it's one of the best groups I've found because people generally are there to provide value to others. But still, with that many people, there are numerous posts every day and dozens and dozens of comments on each post. It's easy to quickly begin to feel wildly confused if not completely invisible.

Facebook made a weird change (what else is new) one week whereby I began getting email notifications each time someone posted in a group I'm a member of. This was beyond annoying. But before I had a chance to turn that setting off, I got an email alerting me of a question someone had posted in this enormous group. This woman had written a book (she hadn't yet published it) as well as created a course, and she was looking for advice on which to launch first.

Oh, and her name was Libby.

Why is that important?

Because, until I was in eighth grade, I was referred to as Libby. And up until that point, I'd only ever met one other Libby in my entire life (the third "Meeting another Libby" experience happened a few months later. She was my barista at Starbucks. Who's surprised?).

Anyway, I knew I could help Libby Number Two sort through the best way to approach her launches. There were already nearly fifty comments in the thread, and it seemed everyone was telling her what to do without asking any questions. I needed a little bit more information before I could confidently give her my two cents.

So I asked her some questions about her topic and her goals, and we began messaging. One of us friend-requested the other, and our conversation moved from the group thread to Facebook messenger. We agreed that it would be a great idea to hop on a phone call to figure out the best approach for her situation.

We scheduled a time to chat later in the week, which got bumped because she got sick. We re-scheduled for the following week.

I called her at the appointed time. Her phone number had a Michigan area code. We began to chat and got along really well. The flow of the conversation was effortless. I told her about my history with the name Libby, we both had a good "what an interesting coincidence" moment, and we moved on. She began telling me her backstory, which was absolutely incredible, and at one point she said, "So at that point we picked up and moved to Phoenix."

I interjected. "Oh, when did you live in Phoenix? I'm in Phoenix," I said.

"I thought so based on your area code," she responded. "We're here now. Well, actually we're not in Phoenix, we're in Buckeye."

"Um, I'm in Buckeye," I said.

Pause.

"You're kidding! We live in Preposterous Pond." I made up this neighborhood name so I don't reveal our actual location, but frankly, it might as well be named Preposterous Pond, and if you know where I live you're no doubt nodding your head in agreement.

"Um...I live in Preposterous Pond," I slowly responded.

Longer pause.

"I live on Devon Street."

I had to sit down.

"Libby, *I live on Devon Street!*"

People, you can't make this shit up.

"Wow," she said. "Well, should we hang up and just meet at the coffee shop?"

"I'll be there in ten minutes," I replied.

Seriously, this woman lives *ten houses from me*!

I've never seen her in the neighborhood grocery story. I've never seen her at Target. Or the neighborhood pool. Or Starbucks. The only way I got in contact with her was through this enormous Facebook group that I almost never participate in when I just happened to chime in on her post because I received a Facebook notification I'd never gotten before. And she and her family ended up moving about forty miles east within a month of that day. They were ten or so houses from me for the exact amount of time necessary for us to meet in person and establish a connection that continues to grow.

That, my friends, is what is meant when people say, "The universe will move things around to ensure that you meet who you need to meet through whatever means necessary."

You better believe I still have a solid daily plan. And I execute like a crazed, focused maniac. But I also have complete and total faith that, even though my ideal everything isn't visibly right here right now, it's exactly where it needs to be, and it will get to me exactly when it's supposed to.

As long as my vibration continues to match that of anything I'm seeking, it's universally impossible for the two *not* to meet. So, in short, it's okay that Joshua Jackson is in a relationship, Betty White doesn't realize how fun it would be to have lunch with me, and there aren't many (okay, any) dolphins I can swim with in the desert. I'm going to keep focusing on vibrating as though he isn't, she does, and there are, and it's all going to work itself out just fine.

In our personal lives, we often work really hard to hold onto people, afraid that the old adage is, in fact, a crock of shit and that if we love something and let it go, it's just gone whether or not it was meant for us. Fact: the people who are meant to be there for more than a season will either stay or return. Period. You won't have to do anything beyond being your authentic self.

When I was in eighth grade, we moved to Buffalo, New York. If there is a worse time to move as a girl, I don't know what it would be. In fact, the first day of eighth grade is exactly when I went from Libby to Liz. A boy named Peter approached me in the cafeteria and asked if I was new.

"Yes," I responded.

"What's your name?" he asked.

"Liz."

Wait...what?

It was already out of my mouth. How do you go back and say, "I mean...Libby." For some reason, I could not say Libby. It made me feel really young. It was a little kid's name. I got off the bus that day, and while casually sauntering past my mother, I said, "Oh, if anyone calls tonight and asks for 'Liz,' that's me."

The poor woman. Honestly.

One of the very best things to happen to me that year was a girl named Natalie. She was everything I aspired to be: gorgeous, smart, kind, humble, and confident. She and I became inseparable. She was my Nat, and I was her Lizard. Until, just after the end of ninth grade, my parents announced that we were moving back to Delaware, where I'd have to explain, among other things, my new name to everyone who'd known me as Libby all my life.

Motherfucker.

Cell phones didn't yet exist, and Facebook likely hadn't yet been dreamed up in Mark Zuckerberg's wildest imagination. And so, Natalie and I understandably drifted apart. She and her family ended up moving to New Jersey after she graduated from high school, and they were only about an hour and a half from me, but I was off to *The Ohio State University* and, again, no cell phones or Facebook.

Fast-forward twenty-five years. Facebook *does* exist, and Natalie and I are Facebook friends, but neither of us had attempted any sort of reconnection. We laugh about this now, as the reasons are both understandable and ridiculous; we each thought the other maybe didn't think as much of the original friendship. We didn't want to be disappointed with a simple and sterile, "Hey. Good to hear from you. Hope all is well" reply. We really wasted a lot of time worrying about something so absurd.

Two years later, Natalie *did* send me a Facebook message. She was coming to Phoenix and wondered if I'd like to get together for coffee. Um, is Chris Pratt just a little bit cute? Hell yes I want to get together for coffee! I was so excited, in fact, that I arrived at her hotel at the exact time we'd agreed upon—four Mondays too early. When the correct date rolled around, Nat sent me a text saying they were running a bit late. Now see, I thought she was here on business. That's the assumption I went in with. But her text said they were running late because they were house hunting.

You're house hunting?

Yes...for my parents.

Ok, but that means you'll be here a lot, right?

Yes, definitely.

Well this is fantastic.

I mean, we're a package deal, so we're looking for houses too.

I can't handle the emotional roller coaster I'm on right now. I thought you were here for business!

Oh yeah. No. Did I not mention this?

No. No you did not.

We agreed to meet up the following day, which was definitely in her best interests as it gave me time to calm down and call my entire family and yell, "NATALIE IS MOVING HERE! NATALIE IS MOVING HERE!" It took everyone a moment to process this because, remember, I hadn't spoken with her in twenty-seven years.

The next day, it was like I'd walked right back into eighth grade at Heim Middle School in Williamsville, NY. I get that you can reconnect with high school friends and be quite happy to see one another and have a lovely chat and be interested in what they're up to and thrilled they're happy and all that jazz, but this was like we'd just experienced a twenty-seven-year wrinkle in time. This girl is *exactly the same*! Our connection is exactly the same! Different stages of life, different lifestyles altogether, but at the core, nothing has changed.

And now she's moving here, and I apologize to her husband, Andrew, in advance because I'm going to be hanging around. Like, a lot. And this is the proof I have for you that the people who are meant to be in your life for the long haul may dip out for a bit, but they'll always return. And you won't have to do a single thing to influence it. Things are always exactly as they are meant to be. And the minute you choose to stop running the wrong way on the moving walkway, you too will discover this to be true.

Everyone (understandably) wants a guarantee that the road they're about to travel will be worth it. They often feel a sense of entitlement when it comes to success and fulfillment and think the whole journey should come with a script, like a movie. To be sure, the journey is much like a movie. But it's usually the kind of move where you are sure that Jerome is the killer until the very last second when it's revealed that the killer is, in fact, Julia. But after you get over your shock, you're thrilled because you really liked Jerome.

Your business and your life won't always end up the way you initially plan. In fact, it almost always will end up *quite* differently. When I started Publish A Profitable Book, it was with a $47 course. Two years later, my main offering is wildly different in every way. I'm still doing what I love, but I'm far more satisfied with the impact I'm making and the relationships I'm building along the way.

No one is going to arrive on your doorstep and hand you a silver platter with all your hopes and dreams on it when you've been sitting in front of Hulu for a week straight meditating on the vision of that happening. At the same time, spending twenty-three hours a day online, trying to force people to connect, and building a business on a shaky foundation won't work either. The key is maintaining a balance between the two.

I truly believe that we meet who we're meant to meet, and people are either a blessing or a lesson. Experiences teach us—or they don't, at which point they're presented differently with the hope that we will learn from them if they're presented differently, much like the new style of math, which makes it ten times more difficult to help my kids with their math homework than it already was. I recently read that everyone we meet and every experience we have is one of two things: a reminder of where we've been or an invitation to something new. The key is to differentiate between the two and not make "coincidences" into more than they are.

For example, if I am thinking about getting married again, and I look up and see a photo of Shemar Moore, it is not necessarily the universe telling me that I'm meant to marry Shemar Moore. (Right?) But we can each look at our lives personally and professionally and realize that there were people who were meant to come into our lives at certain times. We think, "If only I'd met you at a different time" or "If only this opportunity came my way at a different time," and both ideas are lunacy because everything comes when it's supposed to come. It's all about staying in the flow and not forcing. There is a fine line between momentum and force.

TIME TO TAKE ACTION

JOURNAL ACTIVITY

- In what area of your personal and professional lives do you tend to try to force outcomes?
- Why are you resistant to letting them unfold on their own?
- In what ways does this force serve you?
- In what ways does it hinder you?

ENOUGH ALREADY

Well, here we are.

It's ridiculously absurd how challenging it is for me to declare a book titled *Enough* finished. But I have to practice what I preach and honor every single word by saying, "That's all, folks" (for now, anyway).

I wrote this book while living it, and one day recently as I drove through my dream neighborhood in Phoenix, assuming that I was driving toward my beautiful home, I realized that every single one of my wildest dreams both has happened and has yet to happen. It all depends on which version of myself I'm most focused on in any moment. That was a confusing realization at first, and I had to let it sink in so I could properly wrap my brain around it.

As the magical Claire Wineland said, "I think I'm just as confused as everyone else on how to make our lives a piece of art, but I think that part of the joy is simply trying."

Right now, in this moment sitting in The Henry, declaring this book to be enough, I recognize that my own *enough* exists not because I'm the best mom every day or a *New York Times* #1 bestselling author or a successful writing coach or jewelry designer or leather maker or a sarcastic, partially recovered hypochondriac.

It exists because I never quit. Nothing more. Nothing less.

That simple fact ensures that I always have and forever am *enough*.

I have finally learned how to go from *When I Am* to *I Am*. And that simple shift has made all the difference. But man, it was *not* easy.

I leave you with this: Enough is enough. You were enough the minute you were born, and you will continue to be enough indefinitely. The only person standing in the way of your own unique *enough* is you. So step aside. Let that person who's been standing behind you all these years step forward into the light. Honor her. Look at the smile on her face as you simultaneously feel pride swell in your soul. Now, grab her hand, stand proudly alongside her, and say it with me:

Regardless of where I am,
Regardless of what physically surrounds me in any
moment,
I am value.
I am worth.
I am love.

I am exactly where I'm supposed to be.
I am enough.
And I'll grow from here.

ACKNOWLEDGMENTS

It's nearly impossible to describe how full-circle a moment this book represents. I'm profoundly grateful to the people who ushered me along so that the content could be written in the way that it was.

Grace—My beautiful girl, I adore you. You are more self-aware at nineteen than I was at forty. You have *always* been enough. Enough with the tattoos.

Jack—When you were little, "You've Got a Friend in Me" from *Toy Story* was my song for you. It's still perfect; you're everything that is right about a friend, and you're one of the most determined people I've ever known. Enough driving so fast.

Henry—My song for you when you were little was "Forever Young" by Rod Stewart. Amazingly, every word still rings true. Your life imitates the most inspirational piece of art I could ever lay eyes on. Enough with the negotiations.

George—You are, quite simply, one of the funniest people I have ever known with a heart of absolute gold.

Who you are at your core makes my heart smile constantly. Enough with the silverware inspections.

Nina—You are proof of the extraordinary beauty that results when you "Never force; always flow." The universe knew exactly where you were and how to get me to you. Enough with the math wizardry; it makes me feel less than smart. አመሰግናለሁ.

Erin, Heather, Karen, Katie, and Natalie—Thank you for being my tribe. Thank you for believing I was enough even on the days when I didn't want to get out of bed.

Mike—Your friendship is profoundly symbolic to me. Yes, I want to punch you in the throat sometimes, but you will forever remain proof that when you keep the faith, great people show up.

Kirk—Thank you for opening my eyes so many times and for inspiring me through your selfless dedication to your own North Star.

Vann—You kept the visual illustrations prepared, the witty puns coming, and the airplane fueled for emergencies. You are the true definition of a great business partner who can simultaneously be a sincere and lifelong friend.

Julian Rosen and Tommy Baker—Thank you for your support of both this book and me. Your relentless yet compassionate approaches made more of a difference in one year than I ever believed was possible. You are exactly what valuable coaching is all about and the epitome of why everyone should *want* a coach. I still hate burpees.

To each and every one of my clients—Thank you for trusting me with your stories. It has been and will continue to be my honor and privilege to help you get them out into the world so that they may impact others.

Andrea, Breann, Cassie, Celeste, Jackie, Jarrad, Stephen (and, of course, Grace)—Thank you for making my morning Starbucks run the best start to every single day. Also, for not (openly) judging me when I opted to switch to Pumpkin Spice two months earlier than usual this year.

And last but *definitely* not least, to Ellen DeGeneres, Sandra Bullock and Betty White—Thank you for inspiring the meditation/visualization sessions wherein we are all having lunch together. I cannot wait for the reality to manifest in this version of my existence.

About the author

Elizabeth Lyons is an author, speaker, and book coach. Two of her biggest obsessions are backstories and words. She spends her days simply trying to figure it all out—one hour, connection, and cupcake at a time while guiding five kids and at least one dog toward the understanding and fulfillment of their own *enough*.

Her goal is to remind at least one person each day that he or she already *has* and *is* enough, regardless of what external circumstances or voices may say.

You can find out more about Elizabeth and her book writing and coaching programs as well as her podcast at www.ElizabethLyons.com.

Made in the USA
San Bernardino,
CA